THE **Author's** PROFILE

D1361466

THE Author's PROFILE

ASSESSING

WRITING IN

CONTEXT

T E R I   B E A V E R

With a Foreword by Geof Hewitt

STENHOUSE PUBLISHERS
YORK, MAINE

Stenhouse Publishers
www.stenhouse.com

Library of Congress Cataloging-in-Publication Data

Beaver, Teri.
    The author's profile : assessing writing in context / Teri Beaver;
  foreword by Geof Hewitt.
     p. cm.
  Includes bibliographical references.
  ISBN 1-57110-059-8 (acid-free paper)
    1. English language–Rhetoric—Study and teaching.
  2. English language—Ability testing.   3. Report writing—Ability testing.
  4. College prose—Evaluation. I. Title.
PE1404.B38   1998
808′.042′07—dc21   97-39401
                                            CIP

Cover and interior design by Catherine Hawkes/Cat and Mouse
Typeset by Technologies 'N Typography

Manufactured in the United States of America on acid-free paper

03 02 01 00   9 8 7 6 5 4 3 2

For teachers who care enough to truly assess writing
For authors who care enough to use that assessment
For students and teachers at the UNC Laboratory School
And for Bill, without whom The Author's Profile *would not exist*

contents

APPENDIX: AUTHOR'S PROFILE
FORMS 139

I just got off the phone with an actor friend who woefully described his wife's critique of his one-night stand last night in a small café. "She said I played to only some of the audience, and she's right."

"Well," I replied, hoping to comfort, "there's nothing more valuable than honest feedback. But I know it can hurt."

"You've got it a little wrong," he muttered. "Nothing hurts more than valuable feedback."

The principles behind the Author's Profile, applied consistently, take the hurt out of valuable feedback and can provide a scenario where my friend's statement might instead have been "There's nothing better than valuable feedback."

When Teri Beaver describes the nonintrusive but structured observation prompted by the use of "the interlearning assessment tool" and its collaborative development by the faculty at the University of Northern Colorado Laboratory School, my interest is piqued; reading more, I realize that what this community has accomplished is even more important than the tool itself.

The Profile is a handy, off-the-shelf guide to assessment, but it will be even more useful if it is used as a model, and local standards are developed through intense community-wide discussion. The Author's Profile embodies the principles of shared public understanding, if not agreement, on what's important in writing, and it suggests a framework for instruction. Right at the outset, Teri Beaver points out, "Writing tends to be fun if done in a community of people who enjoy writing.

The fun need not end just because the skills of the students must be measured."

As a writer whose paying job provides ongoing opportunities to collaborate with teachers in the design of our state's portfolio-based writing assessment, I am constantly questioning the purpose of assessment, as well as its effect on students. When a teacher announces, "This will be graded," the student is likely to freeze up, and his or her writing become constricted. In other words, confidence evaporates and, with it, the author's voice. The writing may be correct, but it is wooden, without heart. Where on our rubrics do we place that sad state of affairs?

The data generated by large-scale assessments, if considered in context, may be useful, but what are the effects of assessment on the student, both at the moment a writing sample is taken and thereafter? Will the test traumatize the student? If so, what good are the data? If the test itself does not traumatize the student, will he or she later be traumatized by receiving the data? A principal complained to me once that students were "disheartened" on receiving their school's data from our statewide portfolio assessment. I learned later that the community was also disheartened by low SAT verbal scores. Neither set of data should be allowed to dishearten, but the correlation of low scores might suggest a problem.

I believe that *every* student can write with confidence and purpose, and those qualities should drive the writing that is done for assessment. Long before grammar and organization can be fairly assessed, there must be engagement. Writing "prompts" can be helpful for some students; for others prompts dredge up the specter of the five-paragraph essay almost as surely as the word *straitjacket* leads to images of padded cells. If we want students to show their ability to organize information and to write with attention to technical detail, we should give them a broad range of topics, or let them choose from a broad range of papers they have written to demonstrate the required skills. Writers perform best when they are encouraged to address their own interests and concerns and to write for real audiences, *and when they are allowed to fail.* If the writer controls which piece of writing is selected for assessment, he or she can experiment and explore, developing a style that serves the work that is ultimately submitted.

Equally essential is students' being encouraged to pursue writing as a form of discovery, a kind of writing, perhaps, that anticipates no audience at all. This kind of writing, never seen by the teacher, never assessed, might be the "other half" of a full writing curriculum. (In my class, I'd take my students' word for it that they were devoting half of their homework time to such writing on their own, but I would continually ask them about it to be sure it was happening.)

Any fair assessment system tells everyone up front what it is that's being evaluated. When standards are public, when examples of student work illustrate those standards, those being assessed can use the system to evaluate their own work. This is where useful testing and meaningful instruction roll up into a marvelous Möbius strip: the beholder can't determine where one ends and the other begins. The student may not agree with the official judgment, but at least, in knowing the rules, he or she has a basis for disagreement as well as the key to improving future efforts (at least in the eyes of those making the assessment). Gone is the mystery of a machine-scored test where the student makes Number 2 pencil dots on a magnetized form that somehow corresponds to a score that winds up on the permanent record card.

The Author's Profile offers a fair, public, author-centered way to evaluate writing, and at the same time suggests the framework for a comprehensive writing curriculum. As such, it will be useful to any individual author or teacher, and to any community, classroom, school, or school district that wants to begin speaking a common language in the creation or assessment of a piece of writing.

The weakness of off-the-shelf outlines is that they often become irrelevant. Ownership through rigorous give and take is what one loses when adopting such a program. Adapting, or using an off-the-shelf program as a starting point, however, makes marvelous sense. The Author's Profile should be used as a model for writing assessment, a starting place for any teacher, student, or community.

As an assessment program develops, several questions should be asked two or three times each semester:

- Is each author learning and growing?
- What is *not* being assessed, and how do we recognize that?
- Should the assessment standards be changed?

In addition, at least once per semester, groups of teachers using the Profile should meet to determine whether it is achieving its stated purpose *and to discuss its unintended consequences*. It may be that teachers will see evidence that students take their day-to-day writing more seriously (for example, polishing their drafts more carefully) when specific components of student work are systematically listed by genre.

The Author's Profile demonstrates a way to list these components, to enumerate typical expectations for each of the specified writing genres. I especially appreciate that the authors of the Profile allow lack of evidence in any component to render that component "unassessable," not counted in any calculation of scores. Specifically, the "unassessable" score is left blank rather than entered as a zero. In this way it has no effect on the averaging of scores.

The modifications a community or an individual might make each semester to the assessment program can lead to the evolution of wholly new approaches. Let this book be a starting point, not the finished product. Use the plentiful and illustrative student works in this book as fuel for discussion until your own students have written pieces that can be substituted for the examples in this book. Debate and refine the specific components that these student examples illustrate, so the criteria and the standards become your own, specific to your community. And, if you have any doubts that students who work with the Author's Profile make significant progress, read the two case studies in Chapter 5, which sample Curt's and Haley's writing over a two-year period, and note how both writers demonstrate remarkable growth in a very short time.

A major criticism of any standards- and performance-based assessment system is that because fallible human beings, and usually groups of them at that, are judging performance, there's no guarantee of consistency in the scoring. The old multiple-choice test, scored by machine scanners, eliminated virtually all of the human factor—that is, once human beings had devised the questions and debated the "correct" answers. Performance-based assessment encourages students to come up with their own questions and their own answers, in the hope that the exercise will provide a learning experience. But because performance-based assessment programs ask human judgment of highly individual work, they will always be vulnerable when their reliability is compared to that of computer-scored tests. The trade-off—the payoff, really—is what will happen in the classroom and in students' learning when what they are doing in their daily activities is what is valued, and when they understand the standards by which their work will be judged. In all these ways, the Author's Profile can be useful as a model. If the classroom teacher applies standards consistently, students will receive consistent evidence of where they are making progress.

But once we take assessment out of the individual classroom, into situations where results are reported by groups of human readers, the question of human judgment—"reliability"—becomes more troubling. To counter the level of uncertainty inherent in such "subjective" judgments, remember the old injunction regarding testing: "Multiple sources of data! Use multiple sources!" No one test or single "battery" of tests, no one written essay, no one portfolio season, will tell the real story. What do *all* the data suggest? What useful hypotheses do they point to? What are the trends? If the SATs *and* the Author's Profile point to similar problems over three or four years, can you strengthen these needy areas of your writing program?

The process of reaching agreement in the scoring of student work involves an ongoing conversation. To paraphrase Teri Beaver's own words, when it comes to a piece of writing "there should always be room for improvement." But the point is that *we*, not computers, are having that conversation, and the conversation is public. Even students get to participate. No mysteries here. Come and tell us what *you* think good writing is; then, show us!

Ultimately, the student who is a confident writer, who uses writing comfortably as a means of discovery as well as communication, has an excellent chance to become an active participant in a literate democracy. What else is schooling for?

Geof Hewitt

*T*he Author's Profile was designed with the help of faculty at the University of Northern Colorado Laboratory School: Sandy Abernathy, Rob Allen, Steve Austin, Jill Brandsborg, Kay Corbett, Michelle Guerin, Pat Heino, Cheri Isaacson, Waldo Jones, Christy Malnati, Sheryl Muir, Janet Parra, Nancy Richardson, Diane Rochester, Betty Stewart, Ruth Thrun, Rea Trotter, Ray Tschillard, Ann Velaski, Wayne Wagner, Sheila Whalen, Jan Whitman, Linda Witt, Douglas Wurst. Thanks for their commitment, professionalism, and expertise.

Thanks also to the following:

To the authors whose stories were first assessed using the Author's Profile (many are listed in the references at the back of the book).

To Kathleen Milligan, Alan Chestnut, and Julie Wheeler who, through it all, supported and encouraged the design and implementation of the Author's Profile at their school.

To Debbie Powell and her spring 1996 Language Arts Methods class, who rated student stories and gave valuable feedback for improvement of the Profile.

To Teresa McDevitt and Eugene Sheehan, who helped to determine the validity and reliability of the Author's Profile.

To Waldo Jones, who worked diligently with the expository rubric of the Author's Profile, molding and shaping it into a workable tool for him and his high school students.

To Geof Hewitt, Ann Velaski, and others who read through the manuscript, giving helpful feedback.

And to Bill Beaver, whose constant support made a public *Author's Profile* possible.

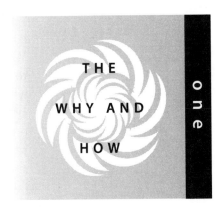

*W*hy another writing assessment tool?

The Author's Profile was developed at the UNC Laboratory School, a K–12 school on the campus of the University of Northern Colorado. Being on a university campus, we always strive to innovate—we want to share the best new ideas with our pre-service teachers, as well as the many in-service teachers who visit. But to be held as an example of what could be, we must be held at the same (or higher) standards as the schools around us. In other words, we can't just focus our sights on innovation, doing things that are new and different without regard to effective teaching and learning. We must be able to measure and prove that what we are doing works. We must set and meet standards for all of our students.

One of the many innovations we have embraced, making it part of our philosophy, is integrated learning. Known by many terms—whole learning, whole language, interdisciplinary learning—integrated learning means the blending of many subjects within a project or activity that has real-life, lasting value.

Once integrated learning began to take hold in our school, we discovered that our old instruments of assessment could no longer meet our needs. How could we continue to pursue integrated learning, which we had found to be of such value, without abandoning thorough, standards-based assessment? We needed alternative assessment tools, and we began with what seemed to be most needed at the time: a tool for assessing writing.

We needed a writing assessment method that could be done in any class (not only English class) by any teacher (not only writing teachers). We needed a writing assessment method that would not require students to spend several class periods on a test that was seemingly unrelated to what they were learning. We needed an assessment method that would allow students to measure and improve their writing skills while working on the real-life, valuable projects that were being assigned in their regular classes. We needed a method that would point out to students and parents what they could do as writers more than what they couldn't do. We needed a method that could be used throughout a student's stay in our school, from kindergarten through high school, and would provide specific feedback that would enable a student to truly grow.

After developing and using the Author's Profile, we've realized that it is more than a writing assessment tool for an integrated learning environment. For Kathleen Milligan, a K–12 principal, "The Author's Profile sets clear standards for student performance in writing and articulates them in a fashion that is helpful for both students and teachers." It can be used as a teaching/planning tool for any teacher who wants to help students improve their reports, projects, or stories (imagine that research paper for the science teacher being used as a tool to guide effective expository writing). "As a first-year teacher," says Ann Velaski, "I found it helpful because it helped to break down the different aspects of writing. I was not confident in my personal background in writing. It was helpful to have a tool to fall back on and say, 'Okay, what do we need work on?'"

The Author's Profile can be used to cut down on testing time and increase learning time (no longer must students spend three periods writing an unrelated paper so it can be analyzed and scored because the important papers they wrote weren't scored thoroughly enough). It can be used to supplement or replace current testing that does not provide enough of the needed details for improving instruction. As a special educator, Ann Velaski finds it "an easy tool to use to set objectives for written goals. All the adults who are involved in a child's case can use the Author's Profile as a communication tool as well. It is clear what the child needs help in without doing separate tests."

The Author's Profile was developed because we needed it to support an innovative program. In developing it, however, we realized that it can also be used to guide effective writing. Even teachers in our school who had previously felt unsure about their skills in teaching writing found they could use the explanations and examples in the Author's Profile to guide their students' writing and assess results. "It approaches writing in all its complexity in a way that respects the process.

This is what really makes it unique and different from other tools," says Milligan.

Since the creation of the Author's Profile, we've realized how many teachers of classes other than English assign writing to students. Burr Adams, a high school math teacher, decided to use it in his classes: "I'm going to score papers twice," he said: "once so they know what to improve and again after their final copy." Language arts teacher Nancy Richardson says that using the Author's Profile "allows for more consistency, because I know other teachers, not just language arts teachers, will be using the same evaluation tool for student writing."

With the Author's Profile, we have been able to address accountability in writing—not just in correct grammar and spelling, but in the writing process as a whole and the skills involved in creating a narrative or expository piece. Results can be summarized and used to evaluate our entire program, and allow "outsiders" to do the same. On an individual level, says Nancy Richardson, "This type of rubric puts the responsibility on the student because it's so clear what the expectations are." Betty Stewart uses the tool in a way similar to Burr Adams. "I teach advanced composition in the high school," she says. "The most valuable thing about the Author's Profile is that kids can see exactly what they're weak on and what their strengths are. It's a great diagnostic tool. I use it for the kids to improve their writing. They turn in the best writing they are capable of at the moment; I grade it using the Author's Profile; then they revise the piece using those guidelines."

The Philosophy Behind the Author's Profile

While much of the process of creating specific facets of the Author's Profile has been collaborative, I have been mainly responsible for its overall development and the writing of this book. At this point, I should set down some of my beliefs—the foundations on which much of the Author's Profile was created. While many of these beliefs are held by many other teachers and administrators at the Laboratory School, the following is by no means a staff philosophical statement. Rather, it is the personal beliefs held by one author, one teacher of writing.

I believe learning is a natural, lifelong process. For writers to grow and flourish, they must be provided an environment in which several things happen, even during test time:

First, writers must be immersed in joyful writing experiences. Writing tends to be fun if it is done in a community of people who enjoy writing. The fun need not end just because the skills of the students must be measured.

Second, writers must participate and collaborate in daily writing experiences. Many classes involve group brainstorming, peer conferencing, and sharing of ideas. Pieces to be assessed can be created in such an environment. Requiring silence or assigned seating in a classroom unused to such an arrangement may actually hinder writing efforts.

Third, writers must make choices. Writing classes that offer unlimited narrative or expository topic choices, that allow students to parade for one another their latest ideas, should not provide a narrow list of choices for assessment. Pieces that are truly measured against standards may be completely different from one another and still provide fair and accurate data.

Fourth, writers must know that their attempts will be celebrated. Knowing that a piece will be assessed shouldn't make the writer feel stressed or worried that he or she may not measure up. Strengths shown in a piece, as well as growth from previous assessments, should be celebrated. Comparisons should not be made between writers, since everyone grows at different rates and in different ways. Writers who are the same age may easily be at different developmental levels in different areas of writing. These levels should be respected. Most important, every writer must be seen as having a next step—something to strive for. Perfection is not a goal, but an impossibility. Mistakes are treasures to learn from, and each writer should strive for personal best.

Fifth, writers (and teachers) must have ample time to write together. An assessment piece need not be timed. Teachers should not be watching clocks or policing for cheaters but creating their own pieces for assessment. What better way to model the idea that assessment is for improvement, not judgment, than for teachers to be eager to learn from their own assessments: "What can I improve?" "I'm eager to see how I've grown." "I worked especially on organization this time."

Sixth, writers must create for real purposes and real audiences. Students should be writing because there is a need for the piece, not because it is "test day" or because the school needs statistics. Whether its purpose is to submit a piece to the class magazine, to add to an author's portfolio, to explain a project, to present an idea, or simply to express oneself, the writing should be used beyond assessment. While sometimes the writer must relinquish a copy of the piece for assessment, the publishing process should not be interrupted. The audience and purpose of the writing should remain intact. While a thorough assessment is a valuable by-product, it should not be the end goal of the writing. The piece itself and why it was created are more important than its rating in an assessment system.

Finally, writers must give and receive ongoing, nonthreatening, relevant, specific feedback. Assessment should happen all the time. It should be expected and appreciated. But the feedback must be *specific* to be useful. A common problem of author's circles comes to mind here. One child shares a piece by reading it aloud and then asks for feedback. A hand shoots up. "I liked it" is the response. Another child agrees: "It was really interesting." Children aren't the only ones who give this kind of feedback, unfortunately. Teachers often mark up a piece to highlight the mechanical errors and then assign it a letter grade. Comments are then added, such as "Nice piece" or "Good work!" How much more valuable this feedback would be if students and teachers have specific, familiar rubrics to which they can refer. "I noticed your problem was much more developed this time." "Your introduction sets the stage, but you could use a stronger hook."

The Author's Profile was designed with the above criteria in mind. It may be used within the context of writing, focusing on writers' facility with various tools. It may be used at any level of writing development, from emergent to professional. Used appropriately, it allows us to learn about writers' strengths and needs without harming their self-concepts or attitudes. It provides detailed, diagnostic information about writers while preserving the positive aspects of personalized, nonthreatening assessment. With it, teachers' goals in writing can move from having *evaluated* writers to having *better* writers.

Use in a Traditional Setting

Though it was developed in an integrated learning environment, the Author's Profile may also be used in a more traditional setting where tests are required. There are benefits to using the Author's Profile, even as a timed, "standardized" test. It gives the writer, the teacher, and the parent a detailed account of how well a writer is using each specific tool (rather than a general score of a category such as content). It also points the writer in the direction of appropriate next steps to strive toward.

The Author's Profile can also point the teacher toward logical next steps in teaching, as well as highlight strong and weak areas in a program. For example, if the assessments of several students showed similar results in certain areas, and the information was entered into a database so that averages could be determined, the teacher would learn what areas need improvement. He or she could then receive further training for a specific area of teaching writing, for example, or invite a teacher who showed strength in that area to teach a guest lesson.

Use Over Time

Periodic administration of the Author's Profile will enable educators to determine approximate developmental levels and degrees of progress for each writer in the use of authors' and editors' tools. Results may be interpreted for an entire program as well, providing valuable information for future planning. In short, use of the Author's Profile provides more than evaluation of existing writing; it promotes and celebrates better writing.

With the Author's Profile, writing assessments can take place in context of the writer's existing program; there is no need to change routines or schedules. At our elementary school, most pieces are assessed using the tool; students are never asked to create writing samples just for the sake of assessment. "Our children never understood why we had to write silently and use special paper," Janet Parra, a first/second grade teacher comments. "It made them nervous to know some stranger was going to look at their writing." But with the Author's Profile, "they just write."

The Author's Profile may be used for any type of writing, both narrative (personal narrative, fantasy, realistic fiction, and the like) and expository (research reports, persuasive essays, lab reports, and so forth). Elementary teachers, high school English teachers, and content area teachers all use it to assess writing. The technique provides guidelines for assessing an assigned report without imposing a single, inflexible format that must be used for every piece in every class.

If the Author's Profile is used once, it provides specific information about the writer's level of development in a variety of skills. Over multiple uses, results can be used to graph the writer's growth over time.

Using the Profile, a teacher can assess a writer's total development as an author, rather than just his or her ability to edit or to select responses. The Author's Profile provides guidelines for self-assessment and suggests next steps for growth.

Because assessment is based on specific standards, rather than grade level norms, writers need not be compared and may be allowed to continue their development without being judged as delayed or accelerated. The standards put forth in the Profile also help provide information for program assessment and target goals.

The Steps Involved

The following is a general description of four steps in the Author's Profile process.

First: The student writes, edits, and revises a narrative or expository piece within the context of any program that uses writing assignments. Ideally, teachers should use the Author's Profile for every piece, and writers should become accustomed to self-assessing every piece using the tool.

The more often the Profile is used, the more improvement is made, and the easier it is to track growth. Even if it is used only yearly, however, the Author's Profile can encourage a student's development as a writer, as well as suggest areas for growth.

While the steps of the writing process may vary from class to class and student to student, the piece assessed should be one that the author has drafted, revised, and independently edited. If a whole program or class is to be assessed, the samples for all writers should be similarly collected.

Second: The piece is assessed for the writer's use of skills and tools. This assessment should be done by the author, the teacher, and/or outside evaluators. Rubrics are provided for rating, and checklists provide opportunity for self- and peer assessment during writing, revision, and/or post-evaluation.

Those evaluating the piece will look for skills in storytelling or researching, such as composing a strong beginning, developing believable characters, and setting the scene (for narrative pieces), or providing a concise introduction, stating the thesis, and supplying supporting details (for expository pieces), as well as proficiency in the conventions of writing—word usage, punctuation, and spelling.

Third: Assessment data is communicated to each author. With periodic administration of the Author's Profile, educators will be able to determine an approximate level of development and degree of progress for each writer's use of each tool or skill.

Data indicating an individual's use of authors' and editors' tools and level of skill may be shared, along with descriptors for each level. Writers can see where they are in their development, as well as where they've come from and what to strive for next.

Preferably, a given assessment will be one of many assessments recorded on the same form, each marked by new dates or numbers, thus providing a sort of graph of growth from piece to piece. (Details on using the forms are provided in the chapters that follow.)

Fourth: Assessment data is generated for the program as a whole. While this step sometimes hinders, rather than supports, instruction, many districts require statistics that can be easily reported and compared. Why replace the Author's Profile with a less effective evaluation, simply because those using it would prefer that it not be "number-crunched"? Developmental levels may be translated into numerical scores and entered into a database for identification of areas where instruction is effective or could be strengthened. At the Laboratory School, we use ClarisWorks for such manipulations, and we are working on developing software of our own. Our ClarisWorks database allows us to organize information by any and all groupings listed on the form's cover sheet (grade, age, teacher, gender, and so forth), provided all blanks are completed and accurately entered for each piece.

In entering data into the database, developmental levels must be translated into numbers. We use the following system:

Nonassessable = leave blank
Emerging   = 1
Developing   = 2
Practicing   = 3
Proficient   = 4
Advanced   = 5

Any time "nonassessable" is recorded, the category is left blank, *not scored as zero*. Nonassessable levels should not be averaged in with other data. If you develop your own database, be sure to set it up so that a blank isn't automatically translated to a zero, skewing results.

Using a database, reports may be generated for individual authors, as well as for teachers, classes, advisors, schools, or other special groups.

Developmental Levels

The following provides a general definition of each developmental level of writing as communicated by the Author's Profile. Each is covered in more detail in Chapters 2, 3, and 4.

- *Nonassessable:* Nonuse of an author's tool or skill may indicate unreadiness, but it may also indicate a choice the writer has made about the appropriateness of the tool for this piece. Therefore, if no attempt has been made to use a tool or skill, the piece should simply be labeled nonassessable for it. No judgments should be made about the student's level of development for that particular tool using only evidence from this piece.
- *Emerging:* When a writer is an emerging user of an author's tool or skill, he or she experiments with it, but shows minimal understanding of its purpose.
- *Developing:* When a writer is a developing user of an author's tool or skill, he or she occasionally (or partially) uses it with some understanding of its intended purpose.
- *Practicing:* When a writer is a practicing user of an author's tool or skill, he or she demonstrates generally appropriate use of many aspects of it.
- *Proficient:* When a writer is a proficient user of an author's tool or skill, he or she generally uses it for its intended purpose.

- *Advanced:* When a writer is an advanced user of an author's tool or skill, he or she uses it expertly throughout the piece, with unique purpose and style.

When to Use the Author's Profile

As mentioned earlier, ideally the Author's Profile is used continually. This results in growth that is easy to track, describe, and encourage. Many of our writers who have self-assessed every piece using the Author's Profile have become more effective writers and begin to set goals for self-improvement. "The students can decide for themselves what they're improving on and what should become a goal," says Doug Wurst, music and elementary teacher. Assessing pieces using the Author's Profile takes time, but instructors who assess many pieces using it become practiced raters, often completing an assessment in five minutes or less. They also become practiced teachers of each tool or skill, as they gain a better understanding of each. As Kathleen Milligan says, "It is both a teaching and a learning tool." For those classrooms for which continual use is impossible or impractical, however, many options are available.

An individual writer or instructor may choose to use the Author's Profile upon completion of certain assignments to determine and improve individual skills and/or classroom instruction.

An instructor may choose to assess only certain facets of writing with the Author's Profile. This option is especially useful for teachers of younger or less experienced writers, or for teachers who are specifically targeting a certain group of skills.

The Author's Profile may be used by any individual, classroom, or school at any time. Conducting an assessment at the beginning of a year may help to plan specific instruction. Assessing at the beginning and end of a year may help to plan instruction and measure subsequent growth. The Author's Profile may also be used midyear to measure levels of development while allowing time to modify instruction. One-time or random assessments, however, especially if they are administered at the end of a year, are less likely to result in instructional improvements. I recommend that assessment be done for a purpose, and that purpose should drive the method of assessment. Once a method is selected, it should be used consistently for all writers in the group being assessed.

What About the Writing Process?

The Author's Profile can be used on any piece of writing, from initial rough draft to polished final copy. If used for formal assessment, the writing sample should be collected at the same stage in the process for every student. Further, writers should engage in a writing process with which they are familiar—a piece to be assessed should never be prepared during a significant change in routine. Even professional authors rely on routines for writing: They often write at the same time and place each day, using similar lighting, listening to similar music, and so forth.

I believe that the optimal time to assess a piece is after a writer has created, edited, and revised a rough draft but before there is any significant teacher or adult help. This is the time when the most can be learned about the author's independent skills. Does this mean conversation and peer conferences must cease while the sample is prepared and collected? Not at all. The expertise of other writers is an important resource. If a writer effectively integrates the advice of others into a piece, he or she is demonstrating a skill used by the best professional authors. Our writing students learn to ask specific questions, such as "Does my conclusion make you think?" or "Do you think I need a new paragraph here?" We encourage them to avoid seeking general help, the kind that passes responsibility to another through such questions as "Can you check this over?" "Is anything spelled wrong?" or the dreaded "Am I done?"

The following are the stages we tend to follow in the writing process. We assess most pieces after the author/peer revision and editing steps, but before writing conferences with a teacher and the final draft.

Prewriting.   Prewriting may include brainstorming, taking notes, webbing, using graphic organizers, discussing, storytelling, or using any other strategy that may help writers develop their ideas or organization for a piece. Collaboration is encouraged.

Use of the Author's Profile is appropriate here as a guide in helping students create a general plan for their pieces. The form, or rubric, for narrative helps them remember to plan such aspects as character and setting; the rubric for expository writing helps them develop a thesis statement and support topics, and reminds them of resource materials to use, emphasizing the importance of selecting a good balance of current, unbiased materials. The author's checklists in the Appendix may become graphic organizers or road maps for story and report planning.

First Draft.   The first draft of a piece may be illustrated, word processed, or written by hand. The focus is on getting ideas down and not on accuracy or neatness. We call this stage the "sloppy copy." Writers are encouraged to share ideas as they're being written, but coauthored pieces should not be used to assess development of individual writers.

The Author's Profile forms can be helpful here, especially if a student is experiencing writer's block. When this happens, we encourage students to change their focus from the problem of what happens next to the form. In reviewing the Author's Profile rubric, they often find that their effort to add more events or lengthen dialogue is actually keeping them from what really needs to be done: developing a solution, adding evidence, or writing an ending or conclusion. Once they begin to work on a new aspect of the piece, their writer's block tends to disappear. Even if they must eventually return to the aspect of the piece that had them stuck, they are able to take a fresh look, handling the problem more easily.

Author and Peer Revision.   Revision involves improving a piece's ideas and organization. It may involve adding details, developing a character or an argument, improving organization, clarifying ideas, and more. The revision process may be individual, collaborative, or both, and an author may seek ideas from peers while revising. Even teachers may give suggestions in response to specific questions. For example, if a student asks, "Is there a better way to say this?" a teacher should respond as coach. Teachers should avoid unsolicited help, such as marking changes on a paper. Regardless of the source of feedback, the final decision of which ideas to include or ignore should lie solely with the author.

As an author works to revise his or her piece, the Author's Profile form becomes even more important. What better way to organize a revision session or a peer conference than to select one item at a time to focus on? The Author's Profile rubric notes these items, as well as detailed criteria for which to strive. If the Profile rubric contains too much information for the student to handle during revision, any one of the three developmentally different author's checklists (see the Appendix) may be used.

Author and Peer Editing.   Editing involves improving the use of the conventions of language in a piece. Here, writers should focus on sentence structure, paragraph development, capitalization, punctuation, and spelling. Resources such as dictionaries and spell checkers may be used during the editing process, as well as peer conferencing.

At this stage, we again encourage students to use the Author's Profile form, as it provides reminders for what should be checked—sentence structure, capitalization, punctuation, spelling, and so forth.

Writers with special needs may require the teacher's help during one or more steps of the writing process. Teachers should determine what help is needed and provide appropriate support. Of course, if the Author's Profile is being used for formal, schoolwide assessment, any adaptations made for individual students should be noted on that student's cover sheet. Special help that may be provided includes everything from providing story starters to writing as an author dictates. Of course, the beginning of a story-starter piece cannot be assessed, and only storytelling and research skills (not writing conventions) can be assessed for a dictated piece.

Some of our young writers find the task of editing a piece too daunting. This provides another opportunity for adaptation. Writers may be asked, for example, to circle but not necessarily correct spelling errors. Others may be asked only to edit what has already been marked for correction.

Final Draft.   Once a piece has been assessed and feedback has been given, students should be provided as much help as appropriate to bring the piece to final form. Remember, the goal in writing is not for students to produce something to be scored, but to create something to be published or communicated in some way (displayed, used to persuade, submitted in a contest, added to a library, given to other authors, and so forth). The writing process continues past the assessment stage.

Assessing a Piece

The Appendix contains forms for assessing narrative and expository pieces, as well as checklists for students who need forms with fewer details. I encourage at least self-assessment of every piece, as well as teacher assessment of as many pieces as possible.

For formal, schoolwide or district-wide assessment, every writer's piece should be assessed by one to three objective evaluators in addition to the writer and the teacher. Each rater should complete a blank Author's Profile form, highlighting perceived levels of development for each area.

While reading each student's piece, all the evaluators (writer, teacher, outside evaluator) should be looking for the author's level of development in each skill. Each piece should be read at least once to evaluate the use of storytelling or reporting skills (detailed in Chapters 2 and 3) and at least once to evaluate the use of writing conventions (detailed in Chapter 4). Levels of development should be selected based strictly on the descriptors provided, regardless of the writer's age or special circumstances. Prefacing the rating with phrases such as "For a five-year-old . . ." or "For an honors English student . . ." should never be done, as the purpose of assessment is to compare an author to a standard, not to other authors the same age.

Once Author's Profile forms have been submitted by evaluators, developmental levels may be translated to numeric scores for entry into a database, if desired. A database can use the writing assessment information to calculate averages for an entire program; a class, instructor, or advisor; age or grade-level groups; or (with permission) ethnic or special needs groups.

Chapters 2, 3, and 4 provide specific directions for assessing narrative and expository pieces using the Author's Profile.

Interpreting Results

When assessment is done as recommended—continually—results can be shown on the Author's Profile forms themselves. (Chapter 5 provides examples of how this is done.) In this way, students, parents, and teachers can review a number of pieces written over a period of time, and can note growth. The forms allow those interested to easily see the writer's strengths and weaknesses, and which skills are developing, on a scale from emerging to advanced.

When each student's piece has been evaluated by the agreed-upon parties, each analysis figures into a consensus evaluation. Consensus may be arrived at through negotiation by the objective committee or by assigning point values to each category assessed and averaging values from each evaluating party. In any case, the final data should be shared with the writer in words, not in points—preferably on the Author's Profile form and accompanied by a cover sheet (see the Appendix).

What's Expected?

The ultimate goal of every writer is to be an advanced user of every author's tool, but this is not expected from school-age children. Remember, the Author's Profile was designed to assess the writing of those with a range of skills, from the youngest emerging writers to professional authors. Remember also that an individual writer may be very skilled in some areas but need work in others—hence the need for assessing each skill separately. Creating a single overall score for a writer would not allow for celebration of more advanced skills and diagnosis of specific needs. Yet at the same time, approximate levels of development may be sought for the various levels of schooling.

It is our hope that every student, upon exiting elementary school, will have attained at least the developing level of the use of most authors' and editors' tools and skills. At this point, writers should show some understanding of each skill and should be beginning to use the skills appropriately.

By the end of middle school, we hope writers will have attained the practicing level of development in most skills. At this point, generally appropriate use of each skill should be shown. Consistency, however, may be lacking.

By high school graduation, we hope for the proficient level of development in most skills. At this point, writers should be using skills consistently and appropriately, though they may lack some of the uniqueness and flair demonstrated by more advanced writers.

At the college level, we hope that writers will fluctuate between proficient and advanced, depending on the skill being assessed. At this point, writers should be using skills consistently and appropriately. They should also be able to use some (but not all) of the skills in such a way that uniqueness and style shine through.

Consistent achievement of the advanced levels of development are expected only from professional authors—and it is doubtful that even this elite group would be rated advanced for every tool, every piece!

Since writing requires risk taking, we at the Laboratory School try not to use Author's Profile results to compare or criticize students. We want students to believe they are writers, they are growing, and everyone has areas of writing they could improve. When reading or sharing any student's Author's Profile, therefore, the focus should be on:

- Progress since previous assessments.
- Strengths displayed by the student as author.
- Level of effort and accuracy in self-assessment.
- Ways to help the student achieve the next level for each skill.

Validity, Reliability, and Bias

When they were asked to use the Author's Profile, our students wanted to know how student-friendly it would be. They asked such questions as "Will I get my piece back?" and "Do we have to be quiet?" and "Who will be looking at this?" Teachers also wanted to know how student-friendly it would be, but they also had questions that reflected their own needs: "How much time will it take?" "Will I be able to use the results at conferences?" Administrators wanted to know if the method was valid, reliable, and unbiased. "Does it measure what we want it to measure?" "Can anybody use it and get the same results?" "Is it fair to all students?"

To measure validity, we tried to compare Author's Profile results to those obtained from other assessments on the same piece. We discovered it was very difficult to compare the Author's Profile with other writing assessments. Other assessments, for example, had different expectations for different grade levels. The Author's Profile provides the same standards for all, expecting students to grow closer to those ultimate standards throughout their career. Other types of assessment provide overall scores for broad areas, such as conventions or organization. The Author's Profile provides specific ratings for individual skills, making it clear what needs to be worked on (for example, not just conventions in general, but capitalization specifically).

Thanks to Teresa McDevitt and Eugene Sheehan, university professors in Educational Psychology, we have been able to check the Author's Profile for reliability and bias. Forty-four pieces, written by students in kindergarten through grade five, boys and girls, from four ethnic groups (African American, Hispanic, Asian, and Caucasian) were studied.

Each piece was rated by three different raters using the Author's Profile. One rater was the student's teacher. The other two were college students who were introduced to the Profile during a thirty-minute training session before being given pieces to assess. Once the pieces were assessed, the data gathered was changed to numerical form for study. We found that although there was a significant difference in scores between kindergarten and fifth-grade students (appropriate for the age span), there was not a significant difference in scores between genders or ethnic groups of the same age. When the scores were grouped and analyzed by classroom, however, we found that students who were in classes that consistently used the Author's Profile were rated up to a full developmental level above those of the same age who had only used it once. Janet Parra stated, "This is a test I can teach to—even practice—and feel good about it. As they use it, they become better writers."

In comparing scores assigned by different raters on the same piece, an overall reliability of .7347 was found. Since I'm not a statistician, this number meant nothing to me. According to Teresa McDevitt, "all correlations are statistically significant." Different raters, in general, report the same results, which is evidence of reliability. The few authors' and editors' skills that showed variance between raters have now been revised for clarity.

In short, though it is difficult to compare the Author's Profile to other forms of writing assessment, our studies show that it does tend to accurately measure the natural development of writers as they mature. Of the samples we studied, the Author's Profile was relatively reliable and unbiased. Further, use of the Author's Profile tends to improve students' use of skills. For me, this information (along with my students' willingness and worry-free attitude about using it) is enough to keep the Author's Profile in my writing class.

 narrative piece can be defined as any writing that tells a story, either fiction or nonfiction. The Author's Profile may be used to assess any narrative piece—fantasy, personal narrative, biography, short story, and so on.

In this chapter, I describe each element involved in narrative forms of writing, including indicators of performance at each level of use (non-assessable, emerging, developing, practicing, proficient, and advanced). Samples of student writing are provided for each level.

No assessment tool is infallible, or even totally objective, and writing can by its nature be especially difficult to evaluate fairly and accurately. When authors, teachers, and raters become familiar with the criteria set forth in this chapter, however, everyone can begin to work toward the same goals. As Lorraine Olson, a Denver writer's workshop trainer, put it, "I finally have a 'test' I can teach to—it actually guides instruction."

Once a rater is familiar with the techniques, he or she should read each piece of narrative writing at least twice: once to assess the elements of storytelling (the literary elements) and once to assess editing (conventions). (Chapter 4 covers the latter, for all types of writing.) Sometimes it is difficult to get past errors in conventions to find the storytelling of the piece, but the two must be rated separately. Regardless of the writer's age or experience, raters should carefully consider the definition of each level, suspend personal judgment, and select the level that best describes the piece being read.

Effective storytelling hooks readers and brings them into a new world. There, they become intimately acquainted with the author's characters, feeling all that they feel—joy, pain, love, fear, anger, excitement . . . Readers also face the problems the literary characters face—problems that develop, worsen, and are finally solved. They feel the release of tension as each problem is solved, though it may not be solved in the way the readers had wished. And finally, they are led back to their own lives, out of the world of the story, with a new feeling of peace, or surprise, or dread. Often, they wish the story would continue; they may even imagine their own sequels.

While many simply marvel at good storytellers and the magic they seem to possess, writers of effective stories use specific elements and techniques in their writing that can be learned.

Beginning

A mature author uses a beginning that will "hook" the reader into the story. Effective beginnings may take many forms: they may provide sudden drama, start in the middle of a scene, give the reader a leisurely entry through description or introduction, jump to the story's conclusion and then fade into the steps leading up to it, plant a question in the reader's mind, or simply introduce the story's narrator. Regardless of the type of beginning, a mature author ensures that the beginning becomes an integral part of the story itself, tightly woven into the fabric of the story.

Nonassessable

A story containing a nonassessable beginning proceeds without introduction. Have you ever begun reading a story and then found yourself turning back to make sure you started on the first page? or checking to see if part of the story was missing? Some authors intentionally begin in the middle of a scene. Many, however, simply build a scene in their mind, without realizing that their words fail to adequately introduce it to their readers. It is not a rater's place to judge an author's decision to leave out an element. Therefore, if a story has no perceived beginning, it should be simply rated nonassessable for that element.

Emily's early story begins in the middle of a scene, with no apparent attempt to bring the reader on board:

"Ooooh mom."
"Go meet the new girl."

"I hate new girls."

"Honey she's about your age."

"Fine."

"Hi, my name is Stefany. You can call me Stef."

"My name is Katie. You can call me Kate . . ."

Miranda's dictated story also begins without introduction:

She is going down the water. There she is. Her name is Sarah. She is dry. She is singing . . .

Emerging

At the emerging level, the beginning somewhat provides an opening to the story. Some stories, especially classic fairy tales, have a standard word or phrase that signals to the reader "My story is starting now!" without using any of the opening techniques that would truly set the stage for the story. In her story, Kathrine uses one of these old favorite lines:

Once upon a time there was a mountain goat named Harry.

Developing Through Advanced

Rating a beginning as being at the developing, practicing, proficient, or advanced level is a matter of recording how many of the following qualities are contained in the beginning of the story:

The beginning sets the stage for the story.   Many different techniques can be used to set the stage for a story. Movie openings come to mind here—especially the ones where the camera pans a scene already in progress and then slowly moves in closer to the action. Words can do the same thing, as in Michael's story:

I wat to a bot ras it was cool! I lik it thar was a oroj bot and a gren bot I lik the gren bot.   *(I went to a boat race. It was cool! I liked it. There was an orange boat and a green boat. I liked the green boat.)*

Other techniques to set the stage for a story include describing the setting through any or all of the five senses (how it looked, sounded, felt, and so forth) or describing the main character through physical attributes, dialogue, or thought.

The beginning hooks the reader.   Prompting readers to ask questions is one way to hook them into reading on. Eli uses this technique, making his readers wonder what his dad's first memory is. Whatever it is, it must be special, and the only way we'll find out is to read the rest of his story:

> **My dad's first memory is the most beautiful one he has ever had, and its beauty increases with age. It was a really cold morning in southwest Louisiana and he was sitting on the shore of the Mermentau River waiting for the east sun to rise . . .**

Sudden drama often hooks a reader, especially if it jolts us into the middle of a scene. Mark's opening line gets our attention in a hurry:

> **Smash. A sudden jolt shot me back in my car seat. We had jest stopped moving. My mom opened the door and unbuckled me. Then as soon as I was free, I jumped for the drivers door to get out. There were two loud clicks. That made me, a baby boy, almost cry.**

The beginning moves smoothly into the body of the story.   This is a difficult skill, especially for young writers, who often manage to write a knock-out first line that is, unfortunately, disconnected from the rest of the story or doesn't deliver what it promises. An effective beginning must be an integral part of the overall story. When weaving a blanket, the first few rows may be beautiful, but the work on them is in vain if they are not solidly connected to the remainder of the piece. If the writer succeeds in making a smooth transition, the reader may not be able to tell when the beginning ends and the body of the story starts. Savanna's piece sets the stage beautifully for a classic conflict between good and evil:

> **Early one morning, the little school bus was trailing down the road. The sun was shining bright, and all of the flowers and all of the trees were blooming with happiness. The little school bus thought that he was the happiest school bus in town UNTIL . . .**
> **The big bad school bus and his gang came to town. Instead of having pretty yellow paint that a normal school bus has, it was black and it had a bandanna around his head. All the kids were mean selfish and rude. Soon the Big Bad School Bus and his gang started to gang up on the little school bus . . .**

Dimma's story sets the stage for her tale as well, setting up the problem, catching the interest of the reader, and then slipping easily to the development of her story:

> **Once upon a time there lived a family of crayons. There was a mother who was yellow, a father who was red, a brother who was blue and there**

was a sister who was purple. The mother was going to have another baby crayon. He was going to be orange. It was only a few days before the baby was born that the trouble began.

It was a nice sunny day, and the crayon family was just getting ready to go out on a walk in the department store. They were just putting on their coats when their crayon box home started to shake.

"Oh, no. I think someone is looking at our home again," said Mother Crayon . . .

The beginning is memorable. A memorable beginning is one that lingers in the mind, even after the story has been read. It's a beginning that is quotable. It may be quotable for the simple reason that one of the above techniques was used so well that it had a lasting effect. Or it may be quotable because of the unforgettable language used, or the emotions evoked by the first line or two. While the word *memorable* may imply some subjectivity, most truly memorable beginnings will reach out and grab you, making you want to find someone to listen while you read them aloud.

Emily's story is an adaptation of the story of Noah's ark, with a special twist you may find yourself repeating. I found myself asking whether Emily's beginning contained a touch of humor or just a healthy dose of childlike ingenuity:

"This is the biggest snow 2000 BC has ever seen!" said Noah.

"What if when it melts, there is a flood," cried Liz.

"Yes it may flood," said Harriet.

"We should build an ark!" yelled Liz.

"We don't have the time to build an ark, we must only build a yacht," said Harriet in a smart way.

"We can't fit all the animals on a yacht!" screeched Liz.

"So we will only bring bugs, and they will evolve into animals," said Noah.

Characters

A mature author describes characters in such a way that the reader is able to enter their lives, feeling their emotions, actions, and needs, and seeing the story from the characters' points of view. The use of detailed, five-sense description, dialogue, gestures and motions, or a single revealing detail may bring reader and characters together.

Nonassessable

If characters are not used in a narrative, this aspect of the piece is nonassessable. Some pieces are simply descriptive in nature—a writer may choose to describe every aspect of a special room, for example. While the piece may not have any visible characters in it, the writer's description of the room may be fascinating. It is not a rater's place to judge an author's decision to leave out an element. Therefore, if a story has no characters, it should be simply rated nonassessable for this storytelling element.

Anna's piece is an example of characters being nonassessable. She projects what life will be like in the future without applying her projection to anyone in particular:

> I think that there will be a lot more people in all parts of the world. Different kinds of people also, more African Americans, and Japanese Americans, and Indian American. People will be a lot smarter in medican and in other areas. There will be a lot more violence and new drugs. They will have to work very hard because there will be very few jobs. There will be alot of different families . . .

Emerging

In a story containing an emerging level of characterization, the writer's words make it somewhat clear about whom the story is written. Have you ever read a story and wondered who it was really about? Maybe events are happening to the narrator and a character at the same time, and you aren't sure where to focus your attention. Characterization is important in maintaining a point of view, and without a point of view the reader becomes confused about what to think of the story's events.

Brian's story has characters, but we're not sure where to direct our attention:

The fish was bedt by sbmaes. The safr was no the taop. The big samaben came and it was explring. The big samaren was going fastr. Tine a big big samaren came. A bote hit a isbrg. And it sild oill.

(The fish was protected by submarines. The surfer was on the top. The big submarine came, and it was exploring. The big submarine was going faster. Then a big big submarine came. A boat hit an iceberg. And it spilled oil.)

Sometimes a story is about an ambiguous "we," and the author never quite clarifies who the "we" is, as in Trevor's story about his trip to Sea World. It is clear that the story is about him, but it must be about others too, his sister being one. Is that all? Are his parents there too?

We went to Sea World. We saw dolphins jump 10 feet in the air. I went to the Shamu show. I got wet after the show. We went to Monsters of the Deep. I saw a barracuda. Then we saw puffer fish. Then my sister saw a great white shark's head. It could swallow a table.

Nichelle's narrative of her experience dissecting a brain is similar. It is clear that she herself is involved, but she is not alone. As her readers get their bearings, they begin to wonder: Who is she working with? Other students? A team of doctors in training? Then, mid-story, another character is introduced—you:

The brain is an amazing organ. We couldn't live without it. I thought dissecting the brain was very fun, interesting, and smelled bad.

The sheep's brain was preserved in alcohol, which made it smell horrible! Once everyone had touched it, the smell went away. If the brain wasn't preserved, it would rot away. If it wasn't for alcohol, we wouldn't be able to dissect things like that.

The sheep's brain felt cold. It was kind of squishy and felt like hard jello. Going through the procedures, we felt different things because we were feeling different parts throughout the brain. Touching the oval shaped brain was really cool. It was cold and soothing to your hands. Feeling a brain of any type of animal is a once in a lifetime experience.

Developing Through Advanced

In the developing, practicing, proficient, and advanced levels of development, skill at characterization begins with overt introduction and description and grows in sophistication to a point where the characters are expertly revealed to the reader—before we know it, reader and character are intimately acquainted.

The main characters are clearly introduced. At the developing level, it becomes clear to the reader who the story is about. Much like when we are at a party where most of the guests are strangers to us, we are comforted when the one person we know best (in this case the storyteller) approaches us with a friend of his or hers and says, in effect, "Reader, let me introduce my friend, Character." Suddenly, we have a person to whom we can direct our attention. We can go on, knowing we are not alone. Eve makes it clear who her story is about:

Ones ther wes a mama dolphin and her baby dolphin the baby oways swem by its mama

(Once there was a mama dolphin and her baby dolphin. The baby always swam by its mama.)

In personal narratives told in the first person, the main character is obvious: it's the storyteller. Young writers often assume that the reader knows them (and also knows any friends of the writer, who may be included in the story) and that therefore no description is necessary. Kelsey makes this assumption in her story "When I Was Just a Baby":

I did not wat my batrol when I was letol. My mom cam wen I was cring. My mom put me in my bad. Sey sade Go to slep. When I got up my mom rakd me. I fall alsepal. My mom pot me in my bed. I sapel for a will but tatn I sremd.

(I did not want my bottle when I was little. My mom came when I was crying. My mom put me in my bed. She said, "Go to sleep." When I got up my mom rocked me. I fell asleep. My mom put me in my bed. I slept for a while, but then I screamed.)

The main characters are clearly described. It is one thing to know who the characters in the story are. It is quite another to know what they're like. Some authors will offer physical descriptions of their characters. Others will describe what the characters are able to do, what they're feeling, how they act, or some combination of descriptors. Regardless of type, all descriptions at the practicing level of development are overt—the character is put on display for the reader. Nikki describes her character by what he likes to do:

Spr Glen likes to hug and ces. He stens you wan you tak a bayt hem rudle. He loves you ef you tak nise and he wil kes you.

(Super Glen likes to hug and kiss. He stings you when you talk about him rudely. He loves you if you talk nice, and he will kiss you.)

Abebech's story (several students wrote about crayons—authors influence each other!) has several characters, but each one is introduced and described so that you can almost predict what they might look like, how they might talk, or how they might behave in certain situations:

Once upon a time there lived six crayons deep in the Amazon jungle, there were all kinds of weird animals and creepy things you could imagined. Their names were, starting from the oldest Mr. Blacky, he was the grandfather, Mr. Cool Blues he was always playing his joyful blues that's how he got his name, next was the one that lighted up just about any room Mr. Yellow he was so bright he had to ware sunglasses, the ballerina of the family was Pinkie she always was tumbling around. One of the crayons that was known all over the animals kingdom was Mr. Red, and last but not least the most loved one was Mrs. Purple.

The characters are revealed (rather than overtly introduced) through action, dialogue, or thought. The more experienced a writer is, the more willing he or she is to allow readers to build their own picture of what a character is like based on the story itself. What a character does can often reveal what that character is like. Actions such as stomping, yelling, and turning red-faced can be used to reveal a character's anger. Stroking a gray beard, shuffling, and hunching over a cane reveal a character's advanced age.

Dialogue can be used to reveal characters as well. Phrases such as "Mom, Tommy's bugging me!" or "Yes sir, I'll have that for you right away" also reveal much about characters, as well as the context in which they find themselves. Whether many examples or a single telling detail are used, stories that paint a reasonably clear picture of a character without simplistically listing characteristics should be rated at the proficient level for characterizaton.

Let's go back to Dimma's crayon story, which begins by simply introducing each character. Throughout the story, Dimma works to reveal the characteristics of each one, beginning with the level-headed father:

> **"Well it will be just a minute before we will be able to go. Nobody wants to buy this old box anyway . . ."**

Brother Crayon, however, looks at life a little differently. He consistently falls apart, rattling on about their family's impending doom and depending on his unflappable sister for his every step:

> **"Oh, no," wailed Brother Crayon, "we escaped, but now Mama and Daddy and the new baby will be used to death. Then later on, the humans will find us and use us too. What are we going to do? This is so scary, oh Sister what are we going to do?"**
>
> **Sister said nothing. Instead, she just sat there with her "are you stupid" look on her face. "Would you just shut up and come with me back to the house before that Diana girl takes Mom and Dad to her First Day of School thing?"**

Characterization is so strong that the reader comes to know each main character intimately. When readers get to know a character so intimately that they readily understand his or her feelings, thoughts, and motives, the author has succeeded in thoroughly developing that character. In the first few paragraphs of his story, Matt had me cheering his character on. Even if I hated spring, I would have been anxious to see Sammy go outside for the first time:

> **"Mom! Come here!" squeaked Sammy the squirrel. "What is it like outside?" "Right now it is very cold." Protested mother. It was the cold season and Sammy couldn't wait until he was old enough to go outside. "In all my 25 children I've never seen a little one so exited about the outside."**

Well, time passed and the cold season ended. So Sammy was as ready to go outside as he had ever been. "Well mom, can I go outside now?" Sammy ask. "Yes." She whispered. "Right now." Sammy rushed into a whole new world he had never seen before. He was so overjoyed that he yelled, "Mother nature, your place is great!"

After his day of exploring, Sammy was so tired he just hit the bed. That night Sammy decided he would escape the burrow and explore his new world farther . . . The people house was a place where many had been but not many had returned. Sammy was not a very brave squirrel, but he was ready to do this.

That night Sammy packed a knapsack with a few acorns, two branches full of raspberries and three pairs of clothes. He set out with a chill on his nose and a longing in his heart.

Matt uses several techniques to reveal Sammy's character. The dialogue reveals that Sammy is quite young, loves to be outside, and is anxious for spring. His mother's comparison of Sammy to his twenty-five brothers and sisters reveals that his excitement is unusual. His actions (rushing, exploring, hitting the bed, packing, setting out) and his feelings (courage, "a chill on his nose and a longing in his heart") all reveal important details about Sammy. None of Sammy's characteristics are overtly described, but as I read the story, I came to know him intimately.

Setting

mature author provides details and images that allow the reader to use as many senses as possible to step into the world of the story. Whether the setting is large or small, it should affect and/or be affected by the characters and events in the story.

Nonassessable

When the setting of a story is not established, it is nonassessable. It is difficult, but possible, for a story to take place in a vacuum. Perhaps character is so important that the setting is irrelevant. In any case, it is not for a rater to judge an author's decision to leave out an element. Therefore, if a story is told without time or place, it should simply be rated nonassessable for setting.

Bianca's story, a written retelling of a book she had read, communicates some idea of the passage of time, but it is impossible to determine when and where the story takes place:

Thea wes A be Bat Thea wes A Paba. Jena oaes wore A ran rabin. He ast Jena Wan do Yuo War That gan Rada. ol the taim. Jeny sen But thes is Not the rai tim. He gav hr Favr's Bot it Din Wort. he ask her aot to the movs Bat it diant wrk. NaoW caN You tel me way You wer that Geen ribn. No i cant it is nat the rat tim. Mene yer's past and JenY aND Jon wr gtting Old. Jeny was geting sik. The dodr Kam. They Jeny sed to Jon to unti the ribn. Wn JooN untid the ribn Jenes hed fil of.

(There was a boy, but there was a problem. Jenny always wears a green ribbon. He asked Jenny, "Why do you wear that green ribbon all the time?"

Jenny said, "But this is not the right time."

He gave her flowers, but that didn't work. He asked her out to the movies, but it didn't work. "Now you can tell me why you wear that green ribbon."

"No, I can't. It is not the right time."

Many years passed and Jenny and John were getting old. Jenny was getting sick. The doctor came. Then Jenny said to John to untie the ribbon. When John untied the ribbon Jenny's head fell off.)

Emerging

In an emerging use of setting, the writer is able to use words to build some understanding of when and where the story takes place. When authors write, a picture begins to form in their head of where the story takes place. Young authors often assume that their readers have the same picture in their minds and fail to (or choose not to) write it into their stories.

Miranda's camping story takes place outside and far from home. It rains, so the reader knows that the story doesn't take place in a snowy environment. So much, however, is left to the reader's imagination. Is it in the woods? The plains? The mountains? What season is it? Is it warm or cool? Different readers may form very different ideas of the story's setting. (Since Miranda's piece was at the nonassessable level for spelling, the following translation was dictated):

Snoopy said to Woodstock, "Let's go camping."

"Okay. Let's pack up our stuff now."

They put their stuff in their car and drove and drove. They found a place to camp for the night.

They woke up. "Let's make breakfast," said Snoopy.

"Okay," said Woodstock. They woke up early!

It was morning. "Let's go find our real place to stay."

"Okay, okay. Let's find the cabin."

Then it rained. "I hate rain," said Woodstock.

"At least we got here," said Snoopy, "and it'll be warm and dry in the cabin."

Another example of an emerging level of setting is one in which the setting (time or place) changes within the piece without an indication of travel or passing time. The difficulty of pivoting between past, present, or future tense is at work here. Young authors especially struggle with this problem, often beginning their stories with "It happened long ago . . ." or "Once there was a . . ." and then switching midstory to events that seem to be happening right now. Matt struggles with this in the first paragraph of his story, as he teeters between present-tense and past-tense verbs:

It's 6:30 I'm half asleep but the excitement is keeping me awake. As I pack the car I can see my father comeing out the front door he's as exited as I am. For I know we are both reedy for action reedy for . . . fishing. As I pack the last few things my father pated me on the shoulder and said "reedy to catch the big one son" I turn look at him and smile not a word just a smile. As we drove off I see my house getting smaler and smaler knowing that today would be diffrent that today would change my life . . .

(It's 6:30. I'm half asleep, but the excitement is keeping me awake. As I pack the car I can see my father coming out the door. He's as excited as I am, for I know we are both ready for action, ready for . . . fishing. As I pack the last few things my father patted me on the shoulder and said, "Ready to catch the big one, Son?" I turn, look at him, and smile. Not a word, just a smile. As we drove off I see my house getting smaller and smaller, knowing that today would be different, that today would change my life . . .)

Developing Through Advanced

As writers become more advanced users of the element of setting, they are able to grow from telling their reader where (and possibly when) their story takes place to painting a vivid picture of their character's world. The ultimate goal is to create a setting that is so well described and believable that readers step into that world, seeing, hearing, and feeling everything around them, as if they had become the character.

The following describes the increasing degrees of proficiency writers may achieve with setting.

The setting is established. At the developing level, the author leaves no doubt when and where the story takes place, even though the information is communicated in a simplistic, straightforward manner. A sense of place may be communicated simply by stating where the story takes place, as in Trevor's first sentence, "We went to Sea World." Conveying a sense of time may be a simple matter of past ("We went to Sea World"), present ("We are at Sea World"), or future ("We're going to Sea World"). Though explained simply, the time and place generally remain consistent throughout the story.

The setting for Rico's story, "The Haunted School Bus," is obviously the present-day mountains, but references to setting are limited:

> Twenty years later two boys named Joe and Bob were riding their bikes in the mountains and found the old school bus. It did not have an engine . . .
>
> The boys found the bus about 20 or 30 miles up the road in an old gas station garage. The bus still did not have an engine.

The setting is clearly described.   At the practicing level, the author goes beyond a straightforward statement of when and where the story takes place and begins to provide descriptions, which help readers paint their own picture of the setting. Visual descriptions, as well as those that convey sounds, smells, and physical sensations are helpful. Curt, for example, tells when his story is happening and then uses sight, sound, and touch to describe a sleepover:

> It was Christmas eve and my friends were over. I was going to sleep when I heard something on the roof. I got up and stepped over my friends in their sleeping bags. They were so close together I tripped over Josh, he woke up. Then everybody woke up because of the sound. Then I told them about the sound I heard.

Abebech's crayon story, according to her first line, takes place "deep in the Amazon jungle, there were all kinds of weird animals and creepy things you could imagine." She further describes her setting in other parts of her story, too:

> The crayon family lived in a very strange place; there were snakes, frogs, fish, monkeys, pigs, birds, ducks, and bugs. It was kind of dangerous place for the crayon family to live in; their wonderful scents attracted the animals, and they wanted to eat the poor crayons.

The setting is believable.   With enough detail, along with cause and effect to explain anything unusual, the more experienced author can convince the reader to suspend judgment and accept the picture being painted, no matter how odd it may seem. Later in his story, for example, Curt and his friends sneak down to the living room of his house. Curt convinces his readers by conveying his own surprise at what he sees (as if to say, "Would I lie about something like this?"):

> So we went down stairs and hid behind the Christmas tree. All ten eyes were on the fire place. Then we saw two black boots, then a body. He was a little man dressed in white and red. He was Santa Claus!

The setting is so well detailed that the reader is able to step into the world of the story.   Have you ever been reading and felt a sudden chill? Looked over your shoulder? Heard a sound? Mature authors develop a setting so detailed and believable that their readers seem to become part of it. They see, hear, feel, smell the setting, which has begun to surround them, rather than to hover before them like a picture. In his story poem, John brings his setting to life:

> **The full moon shone brightly against the pure black sky**
> **The clouds began to drift past sending chills up and down my spine**
> **I heard the long mournful cry of the coyote in the distance**
> **It only set in an eerier feeling than before**
> **The heavy fog held the soggy murky pond water smell around me**
> **I took a step forward and felt the slosh of mud under the soles of my shoes**
> **I walked to the bridge and took a deep breath, trying to calm the feeling**
>   **that someone, something, was watching me, following me**
> **I walked toward my home but was stopped short when my ears picked up**
>   **a sound that alerted me**
> **Footsteps!**
> **Someone *was* following me!**
> **I picked up the pace and began to run**
> **Faster**
> **I had to get to the safety of my own home**
> **As my pace quickened I could hear the footsteps behind me quicken also**
> **Who could it be**
> **Who would follow me**
> **Why was someone trying to scare me**
> **As I ran into the light on the porch**
> **I fumbled briefly with my key**
> **I ran inside and quickly fastened the deadbolt**
> **I was safe**
>   **For now**

Kalinda's nonfiction piece describing her first brain dissection also exemplifies this level:

> **As I walked into Ms. Warner's room I was greeted with a foul, sour stench. I knew immediately what it was. Brains. It wasn't a happy thought. I sat down on my stool fully aware of the smelly trash can behind me.**
>
> **I dreaded the moment when I would have to look at the thing that was sitting in the white tub on the counter. One by one a person from each table was called over with a dissecting pan. Benny volunteered from our group to go over and get the brain. He came back with something in the pan. I was afraid to look. When I did though, it wasn't as bad as I thought it would be. The brain was kind of pinkish brown, and I could immediately**

define the three main parts. The main difference was the size. The brain was much smaller than I thought it would have been. It was only about the size of my fist.

Another smell hit me when Ms. Warner lifted off the lid of the white tub. It was preserving alcohol, better known as formaldehyde. This was the main scent that we would smell through the entire operation.

At last came the hard part. Touching the brain. it took some persuading, but finally I closed my eyes and put out my hand. I was expecting to feel a squishy, gooey mess. What I touched was not that. The surface of the brain was slightly damp but very rubbery and durable. It was weird to touch.

The noises were made mostly by people. There was groaning and mumbling as we came in. As the experiment went on though, all I heard were interested and enthused remarks. I think the experiment was lots of fun. It was something people dreaded but enjoyed in the end.

Problem

 mature author creates some sort of problem for the character(s) and describes it so that tension is felt by the reader. The author then allows the problem to develop, or worsen, before providing a solution that relieves the tension. Whether the tension is caused by conflict between two or more characters, between character(s) and nature, or within a single character, it is a central focus of the story.

Nonassessable

If a piece does not build to a problem, that aspect of the story is non-assessable. Many stories, especially those of young authors, are personal narratives—memories of joyful times, descriptions of special people, and so forth.

Haley's story of her family vacation has no problem, only the joyful memory of a special time in a special place:

Have you ever felt sand so hot it burned your feet? We went to the sand dunes on our vacation. We had fun.

We made dams so the water would stay there. We got dirty. It was fun. Then we slid down the dunes. It was fun.

I got sand up my pants. We had to wash it out. My feet got burned on the hot sand when we climbed up the dunes. We used our hands and feet. We stuck our feet down in the sand to cool them off. We had fun.

We went to our cabin. We came back the next day.

We saw the river, and we made a bigger dam to stop the river.

We made more dams. We climbed more dunes. We had more fun. We went on the rest of our vacation.

Though not a personal narrative, Eve's story about dolphins does not build to a problem either.

Once there was a mama dolphin and her baby dolphin. The baby always swam by its mama. One day the baby dolphin saw another baby dolphin and thought that she should say hi, and she did. One day a girl gave them a bracelet on their beaks. When they went home they decided to play. They played all day and all night until they were grown up.

Emerging

In a piece displaying an emerging sense of the need for a problem or tension in the story, a problem is somewhat clear. This level of development is characterized by pieces in which the characters seem to be facing a problem, but the reader isn't sure exactly what it is or why it's a problem. More often, however, this level is evident in pieces in which the characters face one problem, and then a second, third, and fourth problem. The author knows there's supposed to be a problem but isn't sure how to develop it into a framework for the story as a whole. To illustrate this, consider Erica's entire story, which follows. It presents a challenge for the reader: Which is the story's main problem: Not having crayons? Spilling the crayons? The crayons looking for each other? The missing purple crayon?

Andy was a six year old boy he woke up to the birds singing today was a very special day. Today was Andys first day of first grade he got up got dressed and combed his hair. Hes mom said to "get his little sister" Rachel when he comes down Andy got his old crayons and went to school and he got to school and saw a boy who looked his size and had glasses and he said hello and then the teacher Mrs. honey who had blond hair and pretty said time to read and they read, We are all the same we are all different and after they read. She said excitedly and they lined up and went to the art room and they meet the teacher said hi and she said her name was Miss Frizzel an she had orange curly hair and a purple shirt and a flowed skirt she

(Andy was a six-year-old boy. He woke up to the birds singing. Today was a very special day. Today was Andy's first day of first grade. He got up, got dressed, and combed his hair. His mom said to get his little sister Rachel when he comes down. Andy got his old crayons and went to school.

He got to school and saw a boy who looked his size and had glasses, and he said hello. Then the teacher, Mrs. Honey, who had blond hair and was pretty, said, "Time to read," and they read: "We are all the same. We are all different."

After they read they lined up and went to the art room. They met the teacher. She said hi, and she said her name was Miss Frizzle. She had orange curly hair and a purple shirt and a flowered skirt. She was funny. They painted a picture of the outside of the window.

was funny. And they painted piture of the out side of the window. then in the car Andy said "I need new crayons "and his mom "said ok" and went to Dani's Grocery Store. and when they got there Andy went and saw a big shiney box of crayons he said mom mom I want they's one andy said excitedly so his mom got them when he got home he used the crayons all day. 1 month later. one day he was coloring with his colors and his mom called him and he jumped up and spilt hes crayons all over the floor he ran down the stairs franticly and said mom mom I spilt my crayons all over the floor I was just going to tell you to clean up your room and this might be a good time. to he said ok and ran up stairs mean while the cranyons were looking for each other the blue one found the red cayon meanwhile andy ran up stairs and cleand up his room he found 23 of them but he need 24 he seeched for it every ware it was the purpel crayon and he saw the oter crayons were alive and from then on he lived happeily ever after.

Then in the car Andy said, "I need new crayons," and his mom said, "Okay," and went to Dani's Grocery Store. When they got there Andy went and saw a big shiny box of crayons. "Mom, Mom, I want this one," Andy said excitedly, so his mom got them. When he got home he used the crayons all day.

A month later, he was coloring with his colors, and his mom called him. He jumped up and spilled his crayons all over the floor. He ran down the stairs frantically and said, "Mom, Mom, I spilled my crayons all over the floor."

"I was just going to tell you to clean up your room, and this might be a good time, too."

He said "Okay" and ran upstairs. Meanwhile, the crayons were looking for each other. The blue one found the red crayon. Meanwhile, Andy ran upstairs and cleaned up his room. He found twenty-three of them, but he needed twenty-four. He searched for it everywhere. It was the purple crayon. He saw the other crayons were alive, and from then on he lived happily ever after.)

Developing Through Advanced

Problem creation in narrative writing progresses from simply establishing a problem for the characters to face to developing a believable, memorable, complex problem through a whole sequence of events. Each degree of maturation is described below.

The problem is clearly established.   At the developing level, there is one main problem, and there is no confusion as to what it is. In his Sea World story, Trevor clearly establishes the problem. It happens so quickly that the reader almost has to look twice to discover its importance, but it is unmistakably there.

> **Then we went outside and looked for the sea lions and otters stadium. We looked and looked. We were lost in Sea World.**

The problem is well developed through the relating of events.   At the practicing level of proficiency, the problem becomes a framework for the story. Any events included in the story are there for a purpose: to develop the problem. Some events may help build a premise for the problem. Others may build up to and indicate the problem itself. Others may be included to illustrate the seriousness of the problem or heighten it before it's solved. Remember Dimma's crayon story, which begins with the shaking crayon box? It continues with several events that help to build the problem: escaping from the house. Nothing is included that doesn't help to describe or develop the problem until the crayons find a car door. (The car eventually gets them back to the department store, so this event signals the beginning of the solution.)

"Well it will be just a minute before we will be able to go. Nobody wants to buy this old box anyway," said Father Crayon. However, it was nearly an hour before the bumping of the box stopped.

"Well," said Sister Crayon, "I guess we don't get to go on our walk anymore. It's too late and the store is probably closed by now."

The Crayon family then went out to see what had happened after all of the bumping had stopped. What they saw amazed them when they came out of the box. It was a beautiful home of a human being.

"Wow," said Sister Crayon, "That is amazing. I've never seen anything like it. I think we are in a human home."

"Well, that explains all of the bumping. We must be miles away from the department store. It's way too far to walk and where would we find a home to live in? Unless our next door neighbor, Barbie, will let us move in. And . . ." Brother Crayon was stopped in the middle of his wailing.

"Would you stop your wailing before someone hears you? Just keep quiet until we can find a way out of here," said a very frustrated Sister Crayon.

"Sorry." mumbled Brother Crayon.

The next day, Brother and Sister Crayon started out in search of a way out of the human's house. Their adventure began climbing the stairs to the main floor. That was hard because on the way up, there was a human coming down. She appeared to be the size of an incredibly big Barbie doll. As they were going up, they escaped nearly being stepped on.

The crayon Brother and Sister found out later that the girl's name was Diana. And that the reason that she was moving so fast was because she was going to be late for something called "The First Day of School," and she was missing her crayons in her supply bag.

"Oh no," wailed Brother Crayon, "we escaped, but now Mama and Daddy and the new baby will be used to death. Then later on, the humans will find us and use us too. What are we going to do? This is so scary, oh Sister what are we going to do?"

Sister said nothing. Instead she just sat there with her "are you stupid" look on her face. "Would you just shut up and come with me back to the house before that Diana girl takes Mom and Dad to her First Day of School thing?"

"Sorry Sis, just got a little panicked, that's all," said Brother Crayon.

Sure, Sister Crayon thought. They ran back to the house and luckily, the little girl was still looking for the box, while they ran into the house and told their parents what had happened.

"Well, we'd better evacuate the house right now. Come on everyone, let's go." Said their father. Everyone left and sat down in a worried mood.

"What are we going to do? We got out of the house safely and all, but what if next time we are not so lucky? What will we eat? Are we going to starve to death? What about Ma and the new baby? Is it going to be dead before I even see it? What about me? I'm too young to die. What about Sis and Daddy? If we do live, where will we go? Where will we live? Will we find our way back to the department store? What if we . . .?" Once again, Brother was stopped in the middle of his wailing.

"SHUT UP! WHAT IS YOUR PROBLEM? Do you think we, as in the entire family, would let you, Mom, Dad, me or the new baby starve? You panic to much. You really should calm down," said Sister Crayon.

"Calm down? Me calm down? You are the one who should calm down. The way you're shouting, Ken and Barbie back at the department store could hear you." Said Brother smugly. "I think you have the same temper as the very grumpy rhino living next door to us in the department store," said Brother Crayon with dignity.

"You two stop fighting this minute. It is very juvenile of you to be fighting like two angry bulls in a bull pen. Now come on, I see a door and I think it will lead us out of here." Said Mama Crayon. They found several more doors until they ended up outside. There they saw the door of a car. They just didn't know it. So they got in . . .

The problem is believable. Mature authors include a well-developed problem in their stories, but they also carefully construct it so that it is believable. They convince their readers that the problem actually took place, or that it could have. This does not mean that the problem must be realistic or true, just that the reader is convinced of its possibility. Liz's problem, for example, is so well developed that the reader can almost see it happening. Even if chimpanzees are not really caught in nets, and if chimpanzee fur is not really made into coats, Liz makes us believe that it could happen:

Swinging home he spotted a bunch of his favorite food, bananas! He decided to attack and have a snack. But as soon as he leaped at the bananas he was caught by a net! He tried and tried to escape.

Finally, he grew too tired to try. Suddenly the net began to move down and down until it hit the floor of the jungle!

Soon everyone was staring and poking at him. He didn't like that very much and was wondering why they were doing so.

Soon he over heard the leader of the group saying "Head straight for the coat making company, he'll make a great coat!" He was very frightened for he had heard about that place from his mother.

Oh his mother he thought how frantic she would be and just the thought of her, her loving eyes just everything about her.

He became so sad his eyes began to water and water. He was crying the crying became harder and harder until he couldn't stop . . .

The problem is complex and memorable.   The chimpanzee in Liz's story faced a heartbreaking, but quite simple, problem: He was captured in a net and would soon be killed for his coat. Some stories, however, are more complex. Some offer several problems, but as the story unfolds, a central problem is revealed that has prompted all the others. In other stories, authors use techniques such as foreshadowing to allude to an upcoming problem, encouraging some detective work on the part of the reader; the problem tends to sneak up on them, and rereading the story reveals that the hints were there all along. Still other narratives involve a problem with many angles, one with far-reaching effects, or one that requires some thinking or background knowledge to understand. Such complex problems are usually the most difficult for authors to plan but the most captivating for readers.

Erin based her narrative of a child's life in Nazi Germany on an interview with a German man who had spent his childhood there. The war is clearly the problem in her piece, but it is pervasive through the piece. Its identification cannot be narrowed down to one sentence, it develops into several arms of difficulty, and it does not allow for a clear division between good and evil:

My father came from a family where debating the current politics of Germany in the late twenties and early thirties was a common occurrence. One of his two brothers was a strong supporter of the Nazi party . . . My father's other brother and father were both strongly opposed to the Nazi party and everything it stood for. My father and his mother were both rather apolitical. Neither had strong feelings either for nor against the party which elected Adolf Hitler chancellor of Germany in 1933. Needless to say, my father's family had plenty of heated dinnertime discussions.

During the time that they were in high school, my father and mother met. They did not start dating, however, until after they had graduated. Just two weeks after they began dating, my father received notice that he had been drafted to enter the Nazi army. Due to this, they ended up having a whirlwind courtship and marrying after knowing each other for only about three months. When they said good-bye the morning my father left to report, neither had any idea of what was going to happen to their lives by the time they saw each other again.

During the time that my father was at war, my mother learned that she had to join the local ladies organization which was set up by the Nazi party. They did various kinds of jobs, such as working in the fields since many of the farmers were away at war. Three months after my father left, my mother found out she was pregnant. This was a complete surprise to her—especially considering that my father didn't even know.

Meanwhile, my father was marching into Poland, following Hitler's command to invade. He was sent on several other missions as well. One of those, which he told me about in later life, was after Benito Mussolini was captured by the Americans, my father was one of the men who was sent on the mission to free him. When the troops finally arrived at where Mussolini was being detained, he had already been taken to another location by American guards.

I began life in a small house in East Germany. Things were relatively quiet for my mother and me. I developed a close relationship with my grandparents because at the time I was being raised by a single parent. My grandparents were always there to help out.

After about a year in the army, my father was transferred to the German Air Force. There he was assigned to fly on several bomber missions. During one battle, he was captured by the French and became a prisoner of war, along with several other of his comrades whom he had been in service with.

They were immediately put on a troop transport ship and shipped from Germany to Northern Africa, to the U.S. and back to France. My father received a wide variety of treatment from the soldiers who were organizing the transports. Some of the soldiers were excessively disrespectful and rude to the POW's. In particular, the Americans. It seemed as though they thought the prisoners had lost all human feelings simply because they were Germans.

My father remained with the troop transport for almost five years. When news came that the ship was going to be bombed by the German army, the POW's were taken to France where agreements were made with the French government so that all of the POW's on board would be officially released from the armed services and could return home. Finally, after almost seven years, my father was on his way home.

I remember hearing him tell me his war stories when I was younger, and he said what an eerie feeling it is to know that his own troops were going to be attacking the ship that he was on, putting his life in danger.

By this time I was six and a half years old. We did not know that my father had been captured until much later when he was able to write and tell us. The town where my mother and I lived had been attacked. We lived just outside Berlin in one of the eastern suburbs. We had both survived, but much of the town was left in ruins. The back portion of our house had been severely damaged. My friends and I loved to play in the ruins of the buildings which had not survived. It was always a new adventure because we never knew what we might find. All of the kids in the town loved to play in the ruins. But we received constant warnings about the dangers of our games. Among the debris was barbed wire, sharp pieces of shrapnel, and bombs. Of course, most of the bombs had been detonated already, but there was always a chance of finding one that hadn't already exploded. Our parents and teachers gave us constant reminders of what to do in case anyone was ever hurt, or in case we ever found a bomb. I heard stories of kids who had been playing in the ruins of towns and had been hurt or killed . . .

Solution

A mature author allows the conflict, or problem, in his or her story to build to a climax and then resolves it in such a way that the reader feels a release of tension. The solution is not simple and predictable, but builds over several events, sneaks up and surprises the reader at any time, or provides an unexpected resolution to the problem. Done well, the solution is so integrated with the story that the reader is able to understand and believe (but not necessarily predict) how the problem is solved.

Nonassessable

A solution is nonassessable if the problem (if any) is not solved. If a piece has a nonassessable problem because one does not exist, it also has a nonassessable solution for the same reason. Some authors, however, present a problem but purposely leave it unresolved, leaving the reader to wonder what could have happened. In some stories this is frustrating, and the reader is left unsatisfied. In other stories, however, an unresolved problem is exactly what makes the ending memorable. Rather than judging the appropriateness of the decision not to resolve the problem, any story without resolution should be rated nonassessable.

In Bianca's story, the problem is that her main character, Snoopy, is having nightmares. Her ending hints at a solution but never actually resolves the problem:

Sopeey went to bed. His mom said Good nite Sopeey and soth the door. Sopeey had a dremh. It was good at frst, but then it got skarere. tehn the skare! skare! part kham.

(Snoopy went to bed. His mom said "Good night Snoopy," and shut the door. Snoopy had a dream. It was good at first, but then it got scary. Then the scary! scary! part came.

It went on and on. Sopeey opende one eye, and then he sate boha eyes.

"Help!"

His mom camh in. "Wat is the matre?" said Mom. The baby sared to crye. Wat? side his mom

Snoopy told her, I had a bad drem, and it went like this . . . I had to go acras the old bregt, and it was skare!

"Go bake to bed, Sopeey, and see if thet woks." Sopeey sade awake to make a dream cahr.

It went on and on. Snoopy opened one eye, and then he shut both eyes.

"Help!"

His mom came in. "What is the matter?" said Mom. The baby started to cry. "What?" said his mom.

Snoopy told her, "I had a bad dream, and it went like this . . . I had to go across the old bridge, and it was scary!"

"Go back to bed, Snoopy, and see if that works." Snoopy stayed awake to make a dream catcher.)

Emerging

In a story with an emerging use of solution, the author makes it somewhat clear how the problem is solved. At this point, an author is using words to communicate but is not always communicating all his or her thoughts onto paper. Erica's story presents the problem of having a sister who is annoying. The problem is quite well developed, but the solution (an emotional acceptance of the way her sister is) presents itself so briefly and suddenly that the reader is left wondering exactly how the author could have arrived at it:

She is a plain pest, but she is <u>my</u> sister.

Developing Through Advanced

At more mature levels of development, the solution is clearly established, then more developed, more believable, and more memorable. The following are degrees of development.

The solution is clearly established.   At the developing level, questions may remain in the reader's mind, but he or she can easily see and understand how the problem was solved. The solution is most likely stated directly in a sentence or two. In Colton's story, the problem and solution are both quite clear, though simplistic and predictable:

The hermit crab woes looking for a now shal. The hermit crab saw a shal. But it was to liteil. Then the hermit crab saw a nather shal. But it was to big. Then the hermit crab saw a shal end it was jest the rit siz.

(The hermit crab was looking for a new shell. The hermit crab saw a shell, but it was too little. Then the hermit crab saw another shell, but it was too big. Then the hermit crab saw a shell, and it was just the right size.)

Andy's story has only two sentences: The first is the problem; the last, the resolution:

My dog was to weld for as to caep. We give her away.   *(My dog was too wild for us to keep. We gave her away.)*

The solution is well developed through depiction of events. At the practicing level, the solution is clearly a central part of the story. Events leading up to and developing the problem continue without interruption until they finally lead to a solution—one that leaves the reader satisfied that the problem is logically solved (even though the reader might have liked it to end differently). Liz's chimpanzee, for example, continues to cry, eventually effecting a solution:

> He became so sad his eyes began to water and water. He was crying the crying became harder and harder until he couldn't stop. The group got so sad they cut him free!
>
> At first he didn't realize that he was free he was crying so hard. But he realized that he was free when everybody was yelling things like "You're free" and "Run home!"
>
> He jumped up to where he was before, swung from branch to branch passing the bananas until he got home!

The solution is believable. At the proficient level, an author writes a solution that the reader finds believable. To accomplish this, authors must either work to compose a solution that evolves naturally from the story as constructed or write a surprise solution in such a way that the reader finds it believable.

In Savanna's story, different-colored apples find it very hard to get along, even to the point where one color forces the other color into slavery. Even though the characters (apples??) seem unlikely, Savanna's skill for personification helps us forget that the characters are not human. Her solution, then, becomes quite believable:

> At the meeting they decided that the only way they would stop the slavery would be to have a fight. They made a great plan that day.
>
> They worked long and hard the next day. They had to gather apple leaves. They also had to get apple stems to make their supplies. Many of them practiced shooting apple seeds too.
>
> The next day they put their plan into action. Jonathan was the leader of the green apples. He was armored in tough apple leaves with a helmet made of stems.
>
> The green apples charged. Some green apples shot apple seeds at the red apples. The red apples had no idea what was going on. When they realized, they began to fight back. Apple juice was all over the ground, stems and leaves were flying everywhere. The green apples had won!

The solution is complex and memorable. A solution that is complex and memorable is one that is not easily predictable and the reader is affected by in some way. Readers will eagerly read on to the end of the story and then want to share it with others. Memorable solutions make readers want to laugh, cry, sigh dreamily, or jump to action. Back to Erin's piece about the child growing up in Nazi Germany:

> I will never forget the day my father came home. For all of my life, I had not had a father. My mother explained to me several times where he was and why he wasn't here, but that still didn't bring him back. The first time I saw him, I was overcome with a feeling of thankfulness. I knew people whose fathers and brothers were killed in the war, and even though I had never seen him, I felt a certain connection with my father. It was so overwhelming to see him.
>
> After my father's return home, there were tons of adjustments that everyone had to make. My parents had to get to know each other. Since they had such a short courtship, they never really knew each other before the war.
>
> My father had several physical problems too. He was always tense and somewhat nervous. They believe that this was due to what is today known as post traumatic stress syndrome. That, along with the severe lack of food on the ships, contributed to stomach problems like ulcers, which he still has symptoms of today.
>
> We still lived in the eastern suburb of Berlin, which was now a part of what was known as East Germany. When I was ten years old, we were forced to escape to West Germany because my father had a warrant out for his arrest. The government wanted information from him which he was not willing to give. He got a passport under an assumed name and crossed the border alone. He waited across the border for several months until my mother and I could join him. We had to tell officials that he had deserted us and we didn't know where he was, or else they would have followed us into West Germany looking for him. This was before the Berlin Wall was built, which was why we were able to travel across the border so easily.
>
> Soon after our escape to West Germany, we moved to the United States to truly have a fresh start in life. At that time I was almost twelve. Since then I have been living and going to school in the U.S. I now have a younger sister and brother who were both born after our arrival in America.
>
> It is amazing to me that even though I was a very young child during the war, I still have flashbacks and memories of hearing sirens in the streets or bombers flying overhead. I don't know if I will ever be able to forget the damage that the Second World War caused Germany. I suppose I'm just lucky that my family and I made it through the war so well.

Ending

A mature author provides an ending after the resolution of the piece. He or she may provide a surprise ending that twists away from the more expected resolution, an ending that wraps up loose ends or answers nagging questions, one that circles back in some way to the original or a similar problem, a cliff-hanger that leaves the reader wondering about future events, or a poignant ending that leaves the reader laughing or crying. Regardless of type, an effective ending carries the narrative beyond the solution of the problem and causes the story to linger in the reader's mind.

Nonassessable

If a piece ends without a conclusion, the ending is in the nonassessable category. Young authors will sometimes solve the problem in their stories and then abruptly stop writing, even though there may still be a few loose ends. Other authors will purposely "leave a reader hanging" at the end of the story. It may be difficult to determine whether an ending was left off out of negligence or for effect, so any unconcluded piece should be rated nonassessable.

In Miranda's story about camping, the problem is that it begins to rain and the characters solve the problem by finding shelter. Somehow, however, the solution isn't enough to lend closure to the piece:

> It was morning. "Let's go find our real place to stay."
> "Okay, okay. Let's find the cabin."
> Then it rained. "I hate rain," said Woodstock.
> "At least we got here," said Snoopy, "and it'll be warm and dry in the cabin."

Emerging

In a narrative that shows an emerging sense of ending, the author provides some closure for the piece. In some pieces, the reader is left with an understanding that the story is over but somehow isn't completely satisfied with its conclusion. The problem may have been solved effectively, but something seems missing. Remember Curt's story about the Christmas Eve sleepover where the children actually see Santa Claus? The story continues with one of the boys asking for Santa's autograph while the others quickly escape upstairs. In the morning, the boys wake up with much to say. The ending is surprising and creative, but it needs a bit more for true closure.

> I said, "I had this really cool dream that we saw Santa Claus."
> "I had the same dream," Connor said.
> "Me to," said Clay.
> "I did too," said Seth.
> "Josh, what does this piece of paper say?" I asked.
> "It is Santa Claus's autograph," he answered.

Developing Through Advanced

As authors become more skilled at writing endings, they progress from providing complete, though simple and straightforward, closure to closure that is believable, well developed, and memorable. The following characteristics describe the various types of skill authors may display in their use of endings.

The ending provides closure. An ending, even one that is simplistic and predictable, should provide closure for the reader. At the developing level, the writer leaves the piece feeling satisfied that the story is over. Ben, for example, provides obvious closure to his piece with the following statement:

> **Mi dad's trip wos ovr. Mi mom's trip wos ovr. Mi trip wos over.**
>
> *(My dad's trip was over. My mom's trip was over. My trip was over.)*

The ending is well developed. The next step in writing an effective ending is for the author to continue the events that develop the problem and the solution to the story right on to the ending without having the narrative lose momentum or become too terse or abbreviated. The ending must be developed, not dropped in the reader's lap. Mark strives for this in his story of a car accident. He is the main character, who has fallen into a well. He was rescued from the well, and his family then rushes him to the hospital.

> **After awhile she got tired. So my mom toke over. When she got tired my dad took a turn and on, and on, and on, until three days later they finally got me out of the well. My mom took me to the hospital. They turned me upside down and two gallons of water fell from my mouth. There was to much water in my blood and my heart was working to hard. The doctor**

put a heart monitor on me just in time to see my heart stop and to watch me die.

The ending is believable.   While Mark's story is shocking (and perhaps even memorable), it may leave some readers wondering if the ending could really be true. Other readers may completely reject it: Three days in a well? Two gallons of water? And the obvious question: If you died, how'd you write this story? Authors must work for believability. They want their readers to hang on till the end, but that takes trust. To satisfy their readers, authors must not stray too far from reality unless they can provide a convincing argument within the context of the story that their ending is possible.

Dimma, who wrote a fantasy story about crayons, developed her characters, their problem, and a solution with so much vivid detail that her readers could almost see her ending happening:

After the mother of Diana dropped her off at the First Day of School, the family heard the mother mumble, "I need to get to the department store to buy new crayons for Diana."

They heard the motor start again and they excitedly went to the door to prepare to come out and run in to the store.

When they got to the store, they had to get into the mothers bag so they could be carried in to the store. It was just too far to walk.

"Come on, hurry. We have to get in so none of us gets left behind," said Brother Crayon. He started to help Mother into the bag.

"Stop it. Let your Dad go in first, so he can help us all into the bag," said Mother Crayon.

After they all got into the bag and were seated, Mother Crayon said, "I wish she would get into the store already. I can't stand it in here. It smells too much." The mother kept her small perfume bottle in her purse in case she needed it. Finally she got up and went into the store, with her purse, of course.

All of a sudden, Brother jumped up and said, "I know where we can live! Remember that place on the top floor that was abandoned a long time ago? We can take the elevator up there and fix it up, and live in it!" Said Brother excitedly.

"Well I think that was one of the most intelligent things I have heard. I'm so lucky that it came from my own son," said Mother.

It took a few days to fix up the house that Brother suggested they go live in. But they got it done.

"Well," said Mother, "I think this is a really fine house we have put together. I think that it was just in time, too."

During the days that they had been putting the house together, Mother had her baby. She had gone to the doctor's floor. The baby's name was Orange. Mother had named him proudly. After they had all settled into their new home, they told the new baby the adventures they had while he was in his momma's tummy. The baby was amazed and excited, but had no way to show it. So he just smiled and gurgled.

The ending is memorable.   A memorable ending lingers in readers' minds. They find themselves wanting to read a sequel, or at least another story by the same author. They want to share the ending with someone. What makes an ending special? Perhaps it's the emotions the ending evokes. Perhaps it catches readers by surprise, makes them laugh, or keeps them wondering what would have happened next.

Remember Emily's story about Noah's yacht that was filled with bugs instead of animals to save space? Regardless of how developed and believable Emily's ending may be, her last two lines make it memorable:

> "Land ho!" yelled Noah.
> "Good, these bugs are beginning to bug me."

In Kathrine's story about her parents' divorce, she reveals that every time her parents would fight, she would escape by reading a book. Her ending becomes memorable when she circles back to that detail:

> . . . and then a major fight would break out and me and my sister would just hide in our rooms and read. Eventually, I had already gone through all of my books and then all my sister's.
>
> Every passing Sunday guaranteed a fight, so we all hated Sunday. Even though my parents fought behind closed doors, we still caught a word or two. The fights always ended with my mother crying and my father storming off to the fortress of "his" basement, where he would eat pizza and watch WWF . . .
>
> . . . My parents were actually very peaceful during the divorce. They resolved everything peacefully, and I was amazed at how quick it happened. I think their divorce was easier than their marriage. It sure was easy for me, anyhow.
>
> So anyway, after the divorce, both my parents married cool people, and now I am surprised at how peaceful it is. I am mostly an optimist now, even though my cynic side still shines through sometimes. But my favorite pasttime is still reading a good book in front of the fireplace.

Narration is a difficult form of writing to evaluate. Some teachers try to avoid the task by "respecting students' creativity." Others attempt evaluation, but end up falling into the "red pen trap," correcting errors in spelling and punctuation while ignoring what the story is really about. Teachers who model and cultivate storytelling skills, and make the effort to assess their students' efforts using the guidelines provided in this chapter, will give their students the special, lasting gift of well-equipped authorship.

n expository piece can be defined as any writing that explains or argues a point. The Author's Profile may be used to assess any piece written in expository fashion, including research reports, lab reports, literary analyses, persuasive essays, and so on.

In this chapter, I describe each element of expository writing, including indicators of performance at each level of use (nonassessable, emerging, developing, practicing, proficient, and advanced).

Becoming thoroughly familiar with this rubric will help authors, raters, and teachers write, revise, and evaluate expository pieces with the same goals in mind. As is the case with narrative pieces, in evaluating expository writing, raters should read each piece at least twice: once to assess the elements of structure and content, and once to assess authors' and editors' tools (conventions). (Chapter 4 covers the assessment of writing conventions.) Regardless of the writer's age or experience, raters should carefully consider the definition of each level, suspend personal judgment, and select the level that best describes the piece being read.

In the first section of the Author's Profile rubric for expository writing, pieces are rated for their *structure and organization*—how the information is put together. This makes up the format of the piece, which works as a kind of road map through the argument. Like the wood and nails that must be put together in a certain way to build a house, the introduction, body, conclusion, and format must be carefully combined to create an expository piece that is well structured.

Introduction

A mature author introduces an expository piece in such a way that the reader learns and become interested in the author's topic and what points he or she will use to build an argument. An effective introduction contains a thesis statement, support topics, a hook, and a smooth transition to the rest of the piece.

Nonassessable

If a piece begins without an introduction, that element is, obviously, nonassessable. Whether out of negligence or for effect, an author may begin an expository piece by simply jumping into the research, support, or development of an argument that has not yet been stated.

Sadie, for example, wrote a report on India that included information about its languages, lifestyles, and festivals. Her first sentence jumped into her first support topic, rather than introducing the subject of her report:

India has two languages that are spoken.

Emerging

In a piece demonstrating an emerging sense of introduction, the author provides a hint of an opening for the piece. Emerging authors may introduce a piece with a statement that attempts to get the reader's attention without revealing the main idea of the piece. Many young authors understand they can't jump right into their topic, so they begin a piece by introducing themselves. Katie's report is about gun control:

Hi, my name is Katie. I have two pets, and they are both rabbits.

Developing Through Advanced

Whether it be a research paper or a persuasive essay, when authors reach more mature stages, they begin to learn some techniques for opening an expository paper. They may learn to use some of the techniques before others, but they are listed here in order of importance. If an author uses one of the later elements before mastering a level, they should be checked individually. The piece, however, should be rated only at the highest level for which *all* criteria are met. For example, an author may supply a main idea and a good first line, which are included in the proficient level. If he or she has not also included supporting topics, the piece should be rated at the practicing level, at which all indicators are checked.

Main Idea or Thesis Statement.   At the developing level, the introduction contains either a main idea or a thesis statement, while more advanced levels of development include a thesis statement only. If a paper begins with a main idea, the reader learns what the piece is about. Levi's paper about wolves, for example, might begin with the sentence "I learned about wolves." He would then, in the body of his paper, set down all the facts he learned about wolves. Alternatively, Levi could have started his paper with the statement "Wolves are mammals," in which case the remainder of his paper would have been about all the characteristics that make a wolf a mammal.

A higher level of understanding is evident when a writer uses research to develop an opinion about the topic. That opinion is written as a *thesis statement* (not simply a topic sentence), and the rest of the paper is written to support that opinion. Instead of a lukewarm topic sentence that may or may not invoke thought on the part of his reader, Levi stuck his neck out. He began his report on wolves with this sentence, and then used the facts he learned to support his newfound opinion:

Wolves are some of the most misunderstood animals in the world.

Because thesis statements are an important part of expository writing, they are considered part of the *content* of a piece. While their existence in the introduction is rated here, their quality should be evaluated separately, in their own right. (See the section "Thesis Statement" later in this chapter.)

Support topics.   At the practicing level, the writer outlines a number of points (usually three or more) that are used to support the thesis statement. Since the author is trying to prepare readers for the piece, the support topics should only be listed, not developed. Curtis, in a letter to the president, uses his introduction to list his three support topics. While they are simply stated, it is clear what the remainder of his letter will discuss:

I am very concerned about gangs, guns, and drugs.

Marisa's introductory paragraph presents a thesis statement and support topics related to her defense of the radio, an invention that many would call out of date:

> The radio has been around since the early 1900's and has had a major impact on education in our society. Some of things it has helped us with are the news, traffic, weather, commercials, songs, and entertainment. Even with television and computers, the radio is still valuable technology.

In addition to noting the existence of a statement of support topics, raters must assess their content, which is covered later in this chapter.

Hook.   A "hook" is the technique used by a writer at the proficient level to capture the interest of the reader. Several types of hooks can be used to pique the reader's interest. A quotation can get the piece started, especially if it is from an expert, which adds credibility to the argument. Another way to start is with a brief story. There are other possibilities as well, as shown by our young authors. Michelle, for example, begins with her thesis statement:

> There are too many babies being killed when the babies don't even have a choice.

Connor begins with an interesting detail:

> Saturn has seventeen moons!

Clay begins with a comparison:

> The Mississippi River is like a highway to the people who use it.

Jonny begins with a personal statement:

> Hi, my name is Jonny. I am a drug free kid.

Melinda uses a question:

> What do you think of when you hear the word, "spider?"

In her literary analysis, Erika introduces her topic (a Langston Hughes poem) with a quote from the poem, a thesis statement about what she thinks the poem means, and her subtopics:

> "Life for me ain't been no crystal stair." In Langston Hughes poem, "Mother to Son," the mother is speaking generally to her son about trials of life, hers in particular. At the beginning of this poem, the mother is preparing her son for what she is going to share with him when she says her life hasn't

been a "crystal stair." Langston Hughes describes the mother examining her own life, the mother telling her son not to become discouraged, and the mother not becoming discouraged herself.

Transition.   At the advanced level, an introduction captures readers' interest and prepares them for the body of the piece by including a smooth transition to link it with what is to follow. Luke's introductory paragraph on Voyager I and II contains his thesis statement, support topics, a hook, and a transition that makes his readers want to read on:

> One August morning in 1977, history, tales, and legends would be changed. The second of its kind, was scheduled to go before it's twin. For 176 years they have been waiting. Only now can it be successful in it's purpose in life. The name given to both is very appropriate, for they go farther than the human mind can imagine. Powered by the longest lasting, most powerful force known to man, the twins travel on a highway of discovery on plutonium. Not only designed <u>for</u> discovery for humans, but designed for discovery <u>of</u> humans. This pair, of course, is Voyager I and Voyager II.

Similarly, Matt's introduction brings questions to his readers' mind, encouraging them to read on. Why are Lynx Black Cat irons so revolutionary?

> If you've ever wanted to hit a golf ball with the explosive power of a Howitzer cannon, then this will be the most important article you will ever read. On January 20, Lynx golf industry embarked on what might be the most aggressive sales promotion ever to hit the sport of golf. The new 1997 Lynx Black Cat irons will definitely revolutionize the tradition rich game of golf. Old records will be broken, and history will be made. The club itself looks just like any other club out on the market. But as the old saying goes, don't judge a book by its cover.

Body

The body of a paper, whether it is a simple one-paragraph essay or a thought-provoking doctoral thesis, contains the bulk of the ideas expressed by the author. An effective body will contain supporting topics that are related to the thesis, logically arranged, and smoothly connected to one another.

Nonassessable

In a nonassessable body of an expository piece, no support topics are included. The piece may state a main idea or thesis several ways without building support for it. Or the piece may contain many thesis statements; just when more support could be added, a new thesis is introduced instead. Geoff's piece illustrates this:

> Most people in gangs are on drugs. And all it does is make them more extra mad when ever they get mad. Allot of people know how to make bombs from different countries. And they have killed allot of people. And I have a solution to the problem.

Emerging

At the emerging stage, an author attempts to use the body of his or her expository piece to develop the thesis or main idea with support topics. At this level, writers state a thesis or main idea and try to develop it, but the support for the statement is limited or underdeveloped. If Levi, for example, had made his thesis statement about wolves being misunderstood and then given only one reason this is true, his piece would have been at the emerging level of development—even if he had written several pages of evidence for that one reason.

Kaleb writes an effective piece describing himself. Unfortunately, he begins the piece by asserting in a thesis statement that who he is comes from himself, his friends, his parents, and the media. Then he tells who he is. Only the last paragraph provides evidence connected to his thesis statement, *how* he became who he is:

> I get my self image from myself, friends, parents, and the media, each in a different way. Who I think I am comes from a combination of all of the above.
>
> As a person, I am both sensitive and loving. I am very close to my family and pets. Mia is my dog and Voyager is my cat. I am a good friend because I am loyal and nice to all my friends. I am also spontaneous and fun loving.
>
> My strengths are baseball, computers, piano, singing, and school. My strengths in baseball are pitching, first base, and second base. I also have a very good mental understanding of the game. Working with computers comes easily to me as a well appreciated gift. Music comes easily, as do computers. I can sing and play piano fairly well. While they're not my favorite things to do, they beat school work (by a long shot).
>
> I am lucky because I have a very loving family, Mia (my dog) and Voy-

ager (my cat). Mia is a four year old Golden Retriever, and Voyager is about three and a half years old.

The things I like are baseball, rollerblading, listening to music, computer games, reading, amusement parks, and friends. My favorite bands are 311, No Doubt, Marilyn Manson, Rage Against the Machine, and Nine Inch Nails. My favorite computer game is Dune II, and my favorite book so far is *The Hobbit*. My favorite amusement park is probably Elitch Gardens. My friends are Derek, Crofton, Josh, and Geoff.

Most of the information kids pick up in our society's true, but then there are people who try to give us all the wrong information! They usually do this by calling people "stupid" or "idiot," and just a few people get called "fat." All of this information is false, and the only reason people call others names is to either act cool or to put others down to try to make themselves feel better. I feel that self image information should come directly from parents, siblings, or very, very, very, very, very, very, very, very, very close friends. I feel this way because it is almost always impossible to trust the scum I see on television. If I were to listen to everything I hear that is supposedly cool, I would be nothing even remotely close to what I am right now as I am writing this paper. Instead of being me, Kaleb Parra, I would be a little Homie 'G' Funk who smokes and does drugs. I might even be a criminal cutting school and breaking into somebody's house to rob them of everything they have that has even the slightest value. So, now you see why I think that this information should come from a parent or brother or sister, or at least somebody you trust and not some homie fresh out of the hood. Get my drift? (I sure hope so.)

Matt's subtopics, though well developed and appropriate for a historical look at trains, lack connection to the assertion in his thesis statement that trains provided the first safe way to travel long distances. In this case, changing the thesis statement (perhaps to one similar to those made in the conclusion) may be the best way to revise the piece:

In the early 1800's and even earlier than that, man did not have a safe way to travel long distances. To travel anywhere that was more than twenty miles, stagecoaches and horseback were the only means of transportation. With this era came only robbery, scalpings and the occasional safe trip. On Christmas Day, 1830, the first American rail passenger freight service was opened. Therefore, passengers were not subject to the violent crimes that were once committed before the introduction of the train. This first rail passenger and freight service was built in New York and began operation in Charleston, South Carolina.

American travelers were swept off their feet by this new invention. The idea of safe passage and reliability was all a plus for the newly developed train system. Passengers on the first train sat on hard wooden seats and were often choked in clouds of dust and smoke. The only food that could be obtained on a train was when it stopped at a wayside station. This did not seem to bother anyone. If fact, to travel in the train was a symbol of wealth and class status. The outlaws that had once robbed stagecoaches found themselves out of business, due to the train's speed and pure size.

The first American train was powered by steam, but this seemed only to be "hot air" to some people. In the late 1800's the electric locomotive was introduced. Many people contributed to the development of the electric locomotive. The most famous person to contribute to this development was Thomas Edison. He tested his first locomotive in 1880. Then in 1881, the first electric street railway began operating in Germany. Fourteen years later, America received its own electric railway system in the city of Baltimore.

As time went on and vehicles were introduced, the train may have found its real and best purpose. Railroads haul about one half of the freight in the United States. Railroads also have equal or greater importance in Canada, Europe, and other areas. A train can move every type of material, but they often are best suited for hauling large amounts of heavy materials. This is the main reason that coal, iron ore, grain, lumber, and other heavy products are mainly seen on trains.

The invention of the train has come along way in over one hundred years. For instance, all of today's passenger trains have soft reclining seats, air conditioning, and smoke free cars. Not to mention, all have fine dining for one's enjoyment. Just like every invention that has withstood the test of time, they all change for the better. The train has changed so much that the days of unsafe travel and horsedrawn carriages, are either just a memory or a classic scene in a movie.

Developing Through Advanced

As authors develop their expertise in expository writing, they begin to include in the body of their pieces a reasonable number of support topics (at least three) clearly related to the thesis, in logical order, and connected with smooth transitions.

Remember that at this point the rater is evaluating the organization, not the content, of an expository piece. What is determined in this section, then, is the inclusion and relevance of each support topic, not the thoroughness of their development.

The following describes characteristics of a well-organized body of an expository piece of writing.

The body contains at least three support topics that are clearly related to the thesis. Why at least three support topics? In geometry, two points make only a line. It takes at least one more point to transform this line into any kind of shape. Including more than two support topics will prevent an expository piece from becoming flat and shapeless.

Much like in a narrative piece, where all of the events the author presents should be connected to the problem and solution, the support topics in an expository piece should be connected to the thesis statement. This ensures that the readers' time will not be wasted; nothing in the piece should be without purpose.

Breann's thesis statement is that there are many interesting things about St. Louis. In the body of her paper, she includes three support topics, all of which are clearly related to the interesting things about St. Louis. In fact, Breann has included headings for each section that clearly describe her support topics: "The History of St. Louis"; "The Gateway Arch"; and "Famous People Born in St. Louis."

Support topics are in logical order.   Different authors choose to arrange support topics in different order, depending on their purpose; but they should be in an order that makes sense, given the piece. A chronological order is effective in pieces about topics that develop over time, such as a biography (the life of Louis Pasteur), a historical era (the Holocaust), or stages leading up to an event (the first rocket to the moon). Spatial arrangement works for topics in geography (the Rhine River) as well as physical explanations (how a turbine works, or the layers of the earth). Thematic arrangement works well for topics around issues (abortion, racism).

Curt chose a chronological order for his subtopics, appropriate for his historical account of the Battle of Vicksburg (see Chapter 5). His three subtopics were: What led up to the Battle of Vicksburg; the battle itself; and the effects of the battle.

In Brooks's paper about Sears & Roebuck Company, the thematic arrangement works well:

> Opening a freshly delivered package is a joy everyone has experienced, but it wasn't always like that. Rural Americans first experienced this feeling around the turn of the century, when Sears & Roebuck first offered mail order shopping. Because of the publication of the Sears & Roebuck Co. catalogue Rural America was linked more closely to Industrial America. The catalogue accomplished this in many ways. First, it made shopping more convenient. Second, it made America's rural population feel equal to the more civilized population. Last, it offered new inventions at a low price.
>
> Shopping was made more convenient by the catalogue in many ways. First, it allowed a wider selection than any rural general store. People could buy things that before they would have to travel many miles to find. The catalogue also offered much larger quantities than any general store.

People no longer had to worry about a store selling out. When the government introduced Rural Free Delivery, the first home mail delivery, people no longer had to leave their house to pick up items they needed. The items they needed were delivered right to their door step. This new found convenience truly changed Rural America, by allowing them to buy things they never could before.

The catalogue made rural Americans feel equal to the industrial Americans. The Sears & Roebuck Co. bought in large quantities which in turn allowed them to sell cheaper than any store. Men's suits and fancy women's clothing was easily accessed. Dressing in more civilized clothing naturally made farmers feel more civilized. People could order many things that were not often sold in general stores. Children could order toys. The cheap prices and availability of items allowed the middle class people to collect things that before only upper class people could afford. Often doctors were not readily available to the farmland. The catalogue sold home remedies, elixirs, and electrical devices, which promised cure. The temporary effects of the medicines seemed to lessen the need for doctors in the home. Urban Americans didn't have to travel miles to see a doctor, and now neither did rural Americans.

The catalogue also brought the latest inventions into the farm homes. The sewing machine, for example, allowed people to make or alter clothing much faster than they could before. When sewing machines first went public, they sold for about fifty dollars. Once again the buying capabilities of the Sears & roebuck Co. allowed them to undersell the competition. It also allowed middle-class people to afford them. The catalogue sold the sewing machine for about ten dollars, one fifth the cost. The company sold so many that at one time they were selling one machine a minute. In 1897 Thomas Edison invented the phonograph. This was also made available by the catalogue and was in popular demand. Many homes had one in their parlor, a room used on Sundays where the family relaxed and listened to the phonograph or read the Sears catalogue. The telephone was another invention of which the catalogue sold many. As the technology of the phone became more advanced, the use of the phone within the household became more common, and once again the catalogue provided cheap technology for the common man.

The Sears & Roebuck catalogue changed many things for rural America. Convenient, abundant shopping was introduced. Rural Americans could look and act like urban Americans. The latest technologies were made available to anyone who wanted them. The Sears & Roebuck Co. catalogue brought the civilized world to the doorstep of rural America.

Support topics are connected with smooth transitions. Advanced writers lead their readers through support topics like a guide leads safari members through a jungle—hacking away at any undergrowth that may obstruct the journey, smoothing over any breaches in the path, and reaching a gentle guiding hand over any gaps or changes in terrain. Refer again to Matt's piece on the golf irons. Notice how, after his introduction, the first sentence of each paragraph helps the reader easily slip into Matt's next point:

> To start off with, the Lynx Black Cat irons utilize an amazing piece of technology. This amazing advantage to your golf game is called the Triangular Scoreline Sighting. What that means to you and me is simple. With highlighted scorelines on the face of the club, it allows easier set up and alignment, which give you a more accurate shot. Because the easier you get alligned, the ball will travel more straight.
>
> Along with Triangular Scoreline Sighting came another golf club advantage known as the 360 degree Plus Weight Shifting. To further stabilize the club head, the stability weighted design shifts weight throughout the set. This optimizes each iron's distinctive mass. In the long irons (1, 2, 3, 4, 5) the "notch" is wider and positioned towards the cavity heel, thus allowing more weight to be shifted towards the toe, a common miss hit area in the long iron play.
>
> There are many reasons why you should love this amazing product. Yet the drawbacks may grab your attention more than the club itself. For the most part every person that is going to find a set of golf clubs looks at the price. What you will find with the Lynx Black Cat irons is that they will run you anywhere from $950 to $1,000. Compared to other clubs this may be on the expensive side, but in my opinion you get what you pay for. This may seem expensive to an average golfer, but some experts say, "You play like the clubs you have." Others may preach, "It's not the wand, it's the wizard." Whichever way you look at it the Lynx irons are expensive, and you may want to demo a set before breaking the bank.
>
> If cost is not a problem to you, then you will be excited about the Black Cat's expanded oversize cavity. By the standards of most amateur players, this may be the most exciting development yet. The expanded oversize cavity redistributes 42 grams of steel towards the heel and the toe. This creates an absolute maximum effective hitting area. The undercut cavity enables more mass to be placed at the outer edges of the club head, further increasing the stability of the club.
>
> One last piece of engineering genius that needs to be mentioned is the Acoustic Elastomer ring. Made of hercuprene, a military specification urethane, and weighing only 8 grams, the Acoustic Elastomer ring dampens excessive sound. It also seals and protects the 360 degree undercut from moisture and debris that would otherwise impair the club's performance . . .

Conclusion

At the end of any piece, readers must be able to experience a sense of closure—that the piece through which they have learned about a topic is finished, but the thoughts, actions, or questions evoked by its reading will linger. A mature writer satisfies the reader's need for closure by referring back to the thesis statement, reviewing the support topics used to develop it, using a closure technique to stimulate further thought, and establishing the significance of the message.

Nonassessable

If a piece ends without a conclusion, this element is nonassessable. Abrupt last paragraphs, especially those that seem to be a continuation of the last supporting topic, deprive the reader of a sense of closure. Sadie, for example, reviews India's languages, family life, and festivals. Though her readers learned much from her report, her last paragraph leaves them looking for a missing last page.

> **Another festival is called the festival of the Lamps, and it is celebrated in all the homes by lighting them with a lot of lights.**

Emerging

An author who shows an emerging sense of the need for a conclusion provides some closure for the piece. At this level, the author makes an attempt to end the piece. The reader can tell the piece is finished but is not completely satisfied. Many young writers, for example, end their piece with "I hope you enjoyed my report." While the attempt has been made to conclude the piece, the reader somehow feels cheated. Whitney concludes her report on Incas in this way:

> **The Incas were good workers. The children did not get a name at birth, not until they were 13–14 years. They called themselves "Children of the Sun." The Spanish killed the Inca King. Well I hope you enjoyed my report.**

Clay attempts a conclusion in his report on the Mississippi River. His first sentence could have been a restatement of his thesis, except that his thesis included much more than types of boats:

> **I believe there are many interesting types of boats on the Mississippi. We do not think of ships like these very often since we live in Colorado and have no great river like the Mississippi.**

Developing Through Advanced

Once authors reach more mature levels, they are aware of some techniques for concluding an expository paper—techniques that take more than one sentence to implement. Writers should strive to compose conclusions that contain a reference to the thesis, a review of the support topics, closure techniques, and evidence of the significance of the message.

The following are qualities of well-developed conclusions.

The conclusion contains a reference to the thesis or main idea.   Writers who refer back to their main idea or thesis statement, or provide a summary reminder about the topic give a signal to the reader that they're about to wrap it up. Some writers restate their thesis, while others rephrase it or refer to it in a different way.

Whitney's one-paragraph piece about teleconferencing with a scientist contains a restatement of her thesis:

> I like meeting with dr bob cause I like talking into the mike. I also like it cause he can try to help us with our questions, sometimes his answers dont make alot of cents. But most of our questions cant be answerd so we half to do an experiment ourself and every time we do that he learns something new and so do we. So I guess you can say
> I LIKE IT.

The conclusion contains a review of the support topics.   This goes a step beyond a reference to the thesis statement and requires at least another sentence or two in the conclusion. Authors remind their readers why they believe the statement on which they've built their argument is true. Nicole's conclusion rephrases her thesis and gives (once again) her reasons, or support topics:

> I enjoyed this book because I could relate to the situation. I enjoyed the subtle humor in the book. It showed that the author was a creative and humorous person. This book was not a gripping page turner, by any means. It was a humorous, and sometimes touching, story about a boy discovering himself in a new way.

The conclusion contains closure techniques.   Several techniques may be used to provide closure for an expository piece. Authors may leave a question for the reader to ponder, call the reader to action based on what they've learned from the piece, or end with a story or quotation.

Melinda reviews her support topics for a paper that compares two different kinds of spiders:

Spiders are special and unique in their own way and no one spider is the same, the Dolomedes and Argyroneta prove that. They look different, are from totally different parts of the world, and they live differently. So the next time you see a spider think twice before killing it because there may be something special about it that you don't know.

The conclusion establishes the significance of the message.   Here is where authors answer for their readers the question "So what?" Authors must demonstrate that their thesis statement is not only proven to be true, but also important. The conclusion gives them a chance to convince their readers that their research is more than a class assignment. What they've presented makes a difference. While a nongolfer may not care less about Matt's piece on Lynx Black Cat irons, Matt convinces golfers that his report matters, perhaps even enough to influence their next purchase:

Now that you have the facts about the new Lynx Black Cat irons, the choice is yours. If you want to compromise quality for the price of the Black Cat irons, then these are not the clubs for you. But if a great game is what you are after, consider the irons with all the new technology that could fulfill your dreams of holes in one and great approach shots. The Lynx Black Cat irons are the answer for you.

Assigned Format

*E*nglish teachers are not the only ones who assign expository writing, and the traditional five-paragraph essay is not the only format for an expository piece. The Author's Profile rubric for expository writing contains an "Assigned Format" section for those projects or classes in which a special format is required, such as a lab report, an illustrated book, a literary analysis, and so forth. This section may also be used if a specific presentation format is required: whether the piece must be typed; double-spaced; in a certain font or point size; with a cover page or heading; containing a certain number of words; with tables, graphs, or illustrations.

Because format may change for each assignment, no description is provided for each level of development. Assessment is based on how much of the format was followed and whether or not an author put extra effort into presenting his or her work. Extra effort includes anything that is not required but that enhances (not distracts from) the presentation of the piece: illustrations, photographs, special title page, graphs, charts, and so forth. Rachel, for example, used pictures to illustrate some of the statements in her report about the poison dart frog. Most of her pictures enhanced, and sometimes helped to support, her statements, particularly her use of a map of Brazil and Colombia in the beginning of her paper.

After it has been determined whether an expository piece contains the basic elements in logical order, each element must be rated for its development. The *content* section of the Author's Profile rubric for expository writing is concerned with the "meat" of the paper. Effective expository writing contains thesis statements, support topics, and evidence, all of which are well developed and believable.

If, during the earlier rating of structural and organizational elements, any item was determined to be missing, that element should be marked as nonassessable for content as well.

Thesis Statement

s stated earlier, there is a distinct difference between a main idea and a thesis statement. While both tell what the paper is about, only a thesis statement requires the author to take a risk. Young authors simply announce the subject of their paper, but more experienced authors should strive to develop an *opinion* about that topic—an opinion based on the research done. For authors at this level, raters assessing content should look for a specific, opinion-based, provable thesis statement on a topic of significance.

Nonassessable

If the piece is not clearly written about one topic, it is nonassessable in terms of thesis statement content. For example, the piece may contain several subjects that are not connected by even a topic sentence.

Emerging

At the emerging level, the main idea may be inferred from the piece but is not clearly stated. You've surely read a piece like this before. As you read, you somehow discover what the author is writing about—not because the author has set the topic up for you, but because you have good inferential reading skills. A piece at this level requires the reader to "read between the lines."

In Jacob's piece, for example, the reader can, with some effort, figure out that Jacob must be discussing what he would do if he were the leader of a country. Nowhere in the paragraph, however, is the topic introduced:

> **I would do good to my country. I would do good things to the people. I would go and donate good things to people and things to the poor. I would travel around the world and help people. I would be good to my people.**

Developing Through Advanced

At more mature levels, authors purposely convey their topics to their readers. Beginning with a topic sentence and on through significant thesis statements, developing authors put their ideas on the line, inviting argument and critique.

The following are characteristics of thesis statements in various levels of maturation.

The main idea is clearly stated in a topic sentence.   At the developing level, a topic sentence tells readers what the remainder of the paper will address. To be rated at the developing level, an author's topic sentence must be part of the introduction. If stated clearly, the topic of the paper will be obvious, as in Brittany's piece:

> **Ducks are birds that live in the water and are related to swans and geese.**

The thesis statement is specific and opinion-based.   The opinion-based aspect of a thesis statement is what distinguishes it from a topic sentence. At this point, the author has invested enough time and care in the topic to have developed a personal opinion about it. The author has grown beyond having studied a topic and has begun to feel a certain ownership of it. This does not mean that a statement such as "Ducks are interesting" would pass as a thesis statement. To be at the practicing level of development, the statement must be specific, taking on a narrowed aspect of the broader topic.

In his essay on black Americans, Brendon narrows his topic to one aspect of black Americans: education. Then he takes a stand, stating his opinion about black Americans and education:

> **No minority in the United States has shown greater interest and respect in education than black Americans.**

The thesis statement is provable.   A good thesis statement provokes an "Oh yeah? Prove it!" attitude from a reader. This argument between reader and writer is often what maintains interest. Whether a rater agrees with a thesis statement or not, a thesis statement must be one for which an argument can be built. There must be the possibility that facts can be woven together in such a way that the reader can be convinced.

Statements in the superlative, using such terms as "best," "only," "no other," and the like, leave an author unprotected, unable to convince beyond a reasonable doubt. How can Brendon prove that *no* minority shows greater interest and respect in education than black Americans? He has put himself in a position of having to research every minority, not just blacks. And where can he find data that comparatively measures the intangible qualities of respect and interest?

Levi also risks an argument with his reader:

Wolves are some of the most misunderstood animals in the world.

Here, Levi has put his opinion on the line, knowing he will need to spend the rest of his paper convincing the reader that his statement is true. Using a qualifier—"some of"—saves Levi from having to compare wolves with every other species. To prove his thesis, then, Levi needs only to cite and correct common misunderstandings about wolves. Whether he actually does so or not, it is *possible* to build an argument to support this thesis statement

The thesis statement is significant.   To write a significant thesis statement, an author must first choose a significant topic, one that has the potential to change our lives or our way of thinking. The author cannot assume, however, that the reader will be instantly aware of the topic's significance. That's where the thesis statement comes in. An advanced content-area writer can hone in on a specific, opinion-based thesis statement that will answer the question "Who cares?" even before it is asked.

Different topics are important to different people, so this level of content skill can be difficult to assess. Whether or not the rater deems the topic important is not what matters; what needs to be considered is whether the author has selected a larger audience (a school, a city, an organization, society as a whole) and communicated the topic's significance to that audience.

In his paper, Jonny communicates his personal worry about drugs, but he broadens that worry to society as a whole, touching on an issue of concern and indicating the topic's significance:

I am worried that I might be pressured to take drugs. Too many people are dying because kids have been pressured to take drugs.

Support Topics

*T*he existence of at least three support topics was noted when assessing the structural/organizational qualities of the pieces. Now it is time to rate the quality and development of those support topics. A writer's support topics should develop the thesis, be believable, and should examine and connect ideas creatively.

Nonassessable

If no support topics are included, this aspect of the content is to be rated nonassessable. Some writers provide a topic sentence and then state it again in a variety of ways, never providing the support needed to support or further develop it. Others state one topic sentence after another, with no supporting evidence for any. Still others state the thesis and then jump immediately into a sea of evidence to prove it, neglecting the reader's need for the evidence to be organized into subtopics.

Rico's mock campaign speech, for example, contains a variety of theses:

> **If I was president I would ask the state for some money so I could buy more security at airports so no one can take a bomb or gun on an airplane. I would also use the money to get dogs to work in airports to tell if some one was going to try to take drugs on an airplane and I would try to get more security at airforce bases so a spy could not get in airforce bases.**

Emerging

An author showing an emerging grasp of content in support topics makes at least an attempt to support the thesis or main idea. At this level, some development of the thesis is evident, even if the piece is only one paragraph long and gives just one or two reasons why the author believes the thesis is true.

In his thesis statement, Matthew claims that he is "getting better at avoiding procrastination through hard work." He provides one paragraph of support, in which he reveals two reasons for his victory over procrastination: organization and strict parents.

> **Procrastination, ancient Chinese art, or pure habit? Legend says that procrastination is derived from the ancient smart guy named "Lazyman," the ruler and founder of "Lazyoist," the ancient art of procrastination. If this is true, I could be next in line for the throne. To be serious, I am**

probably one of the worst procrastinators in the world. My motto is, "Why do it today when I can do it tomorrow?" This has caused many troubles for me, such as bad grades and bad work habits. However, I am getting better at avoiding procrastination through hard work. I am getting better grades and my work habits are improving.

There are several good techniques that have helped me change my procrastination; the biggest one is organization. It is much easier to get my work done when I know what needs to be done. The major thing that helped me to become organized was a daily calendar. This was great because it helped me establish a time line so that I could prioritize all of my activities. Another thing that changed my habit of procrastination into one of perseverance was the strict nature of my parents. They would push me until I would get my work done. My parents' support was great because I would get my work done and then I would feel good about myself.

Organization led to better study habits and to better grades, but it ultimately led me to believe in myself. I feel that I have overcome the doom of procrastination. Well maybe not—I'll decide tomorrow.

Developing Through Advanced

At more mature levels, the author is able to develop the thesis into a complete paper. A foundation is built to support and maintain the thesis.

The following are characteristics of more advanced support topics.

At least three support topics are included.   If the body of a piece was found to contain at least three support topics when structure and organization were considered, the piece should also be rated as at least at the developing stage for content of support topics.

Jonathan uses five support topics (history of computers, knowledge, education, communication, jobs) in his paper, which asserts that computers "had a huge impact on our society in almost every way":

> The first computers, or the "beginning of the technological age," had a huge impact on our society in almost every way. There are many ways computers have affected our society, including: education, business, communication, and entertainment. This report will mainly focus on knowledge and education.
>
> The first computers were *extremely* slow compared to today's standards. They had a very minimum capacity, making them capable of running only one or two programs. But in that time, it was a new beginning. Engineers began to imagine the possibilities. They dreamed of a new era where everything was running by computers. People would no longer have to work.

As time passed, and new companies entered the computer business, computers were becoming faster and bigger in capacity. One company would have a "break-through" system, and another company would top it. This has gone on until today. Computers keep getting better and better. It is so amazing how in such little time, computers get so much better than before.

One of the main reasons computers were invented was for knowledge purposes. The computer interested many people to learn to use a machine, because before that, not too many people used machines. Many people began to type too. Before, there were typewriters, yet not to many people used them. People could now type papers, instead of writing them. For some people, typing also became a faster way of getting papers done, then writing them did.

Eventually, educational programs could be used on the computer. Programs for preschool levels, to college and business levels.

After a while, another advancement came out for the computer. The Information Super Highway, or the Internet. The Internet was the biggest break-through as far as knowledge. People could learn more about any single thing they wanted to on the Internet. Not only that, but people could communicate which each other from all over the world.

About 90% of the jobs in the world probably use computers. Most businesses file their records and other things on a computer. Many businesses just have to do with being on a computer all day long.

As you can notice, the world is turning into computers. Almost everyone today has a computer. Who knows, maybe someday most jobs will be ran by computers.

Each support topic develops the thesis. When considering the structure and organization of a piece, raters assess support topics in terms of their relevance to the thesis. When considering their content, raters go further, rating the support topics' effectiveness in developing the writer's thesis. To develop the thesis, a support topic should bring the thesis to life, giving it more depth and meaning.

Even though his piece is only one paragraph long and does not include evidence for each support topic, Jacob's piece on being a good citizen asserts a thesis and then provides support topics that show what he means by that thesis:

You should be a good citizen at school and at home. I think that when you go to recess you should be nice to other people. When you go to lunch you should eat properly. Be cool to your friends. At home you should help your mom and dad. You shouldn't whine. Pick up your mess. You help your country by being a good citizen.

In her article about the movie, *Evita*, Lynn provides the thesis statement that the movie was "well worth the wait." The statement is opinion based, causing the reader to say, "Oh yeah? Prove it." Several of Lynn's support topics (which are actually thesis statements for their own separate paragraphs) show what Lynn means by "worth the wait." Each relates back to the thesis and provides reasons for Lynn's opinion:

Evita has been one of the most anticipated and critically acclaimed movies of the year. It received three Golden Globe awards, including Best Song "You Must Love me," Best Actress, Madonna, and Best Film. It has finally arrived in Greeley, and this movie was well worth the wait.

This movie, based on the Broadway musical by Andrew Lloyd Webber, is based on the life of Eva Duarte de Peron, the wife of Argentine Dictator Juan Peron. *Evita* stars Madonna as Eva, Antonio Banderas as Che, Jonathan Pryce as Colonel Peron, and Jimmy Nail as Augustin Magaldi.

Madonna shines as the famous first lady. Her passionate and moving performance definitely earned her the Best Actress Golden Globe. Given her performance, there is no reason for her to be left off of the Academy Awards nominations, except to say that this is typical Hollywood. Two years ago, Barbara Striesand was snubbed from the Best Director category for no apparent reason accept that she was supposed to be the first woman to be nominated for the honor. Madonna's name was probably absent from the list because of the controversy that always surrounds her. This is truly appalling for an organization whose purpose is to support greatness in *all* aspects of the film industry to be so blatantly hypocritical.

From start to finish Madonna becomes Eva, right down to the brown contact lenses she wears for the role and the gesturing to the people that Evita was famous for. Madonna received a great deal of voice training prior to filming in order to handle the musical aspects of the role. It definitely paid off. Not only is her voice amazing, but the movie's soundtrack has been on the Billboard charts since its release in December.

Perhaps one of the most surprising and entertaining parts of this movie was Banderas' performance. Many were skeptical of the casting move, as the role of Che is an important role both to the story and the music. From the minute he appears on the screen, however, the audience makes two realizations: 1) "Wow, Antonio Banderas can really sing," 2) "He is an outstanding actor."

The character of Che, which was created by Webber for the musical, has an interesting relationship with Ms. Peron. Che shows up wherever Eva is. When she is living with Magaldi, he is the landlord, when she is in a bar, he is the bartender, when she travels as First Lady, he is always there as a "Peron Supporter."

The only one-on-one contact between Eva and Che occurs near the end of the movie when Eva is undergoing surgery for cancer. In a dream, Eva and Che discuss her position in the Argentine government and her life. The song, though it is not new, is portrayed quite differently in the Broadway production. However, Allan Parker made a good and interesting decision in his direction of this scene. Through this scene it is truly conceivable that the character of Che is not really a person, but a physical representation of Eva's conscience.

Pryce was very good as Juan Peron. It would have been easy for Pryce to be out done by the performances of Madonna and Banderas, but that did not happen. Though Pryce's performance was not quite at the caliber of the two other stars, he definitely held his own on the screen.

The movie is entirely music, written by Webber with lyrics by Tim Rice. The score contains several new songs which Webber and Rice reunited to write. The songs, "You Must Love Me," and "The Lady's Got Potential" are strong, moving and fun additions to an already outstanding score.

Overall, the movie was better than the stage version for several reasons. First Madonna was a thousand times better than the woman who played Eva in the company that came to Greeley two years ago. Madonna's voice was actually pleasant to listen to, and she was much more believable in the role of the Argentine heroine. Secondly, this story, to a large extent, is about the locations, Argentina and Europe. Because of the wonderful art of cinematography, Parker is able to move the movie throughout Argentina and then to Europe.

In sharp contrast to the stage version is the movie version of the song "A New Argentina." The scene takes place in the bedroom of Eva and Juan in the play. They are surrounded by people carrying torches and shouting for reform, while all the time standing beside their bed. In the movie the scene is much different and much more convincing. The song begins with Peron being arrested and continues with Eva marching around the country to get him released from prison.

This movie is amazing. You all should see this movie at least once if not two or three times. Madonna has put her heart and soul into this performance and she deserved to have her efforts rewarded by the Academy.

Each support topic is believable.   To be believable, a support topic must be both provable and valid. A support topic is *provable* when enough evidence *could be* provided to convince a reader that the support topic is true, but not necessarily that this particular author actually proved the point. Outlandish claims are usually not provable. A support topic is *valid* when it truly supports what the author intends it to support. For example, would a movie proven to be entirely music necessarily become a movie "definitely not to miss"? People who dislike music would much rather miss the movie than sit through two hours of singing.

To be rated at the proficient level, a piece must have support topics that are both provable and valid, as in Kendra's book review of the young adult novel *Flour Babies*. As you read her piece, remember to judge whether each support topic is *provable* rather than whether each is in fact *proven*.

This story, Flour Babies, was about child care and life when a parent has left. There were two plots. One plot is the care and responsibility of a small child. Another plot is what it is like to be left by a father. This book tells the emotions a person goes through when a parent has left. It shows what torment a person goes through trying to find why his father left. This book explains what anguish one lives with trying to find logic in an illogical place. It also tells about trying to find an excuse for a father to leave.

The author of this story developed the characters very well. The author was very descriptive, using her words as a paint brush to paint clear images in my mind. The author, Anne Fine, also did a wonderful job of not writing down to her readers. Most authors write down to young adults, when we can understand more than they think. Her words were at a level of understanding for most. The language was sophisticated, yet comprehensible. Anne Fine did a wonderful job of foreshadowing and dropping hints. She showed clearly what information was important to remember and what was not. Anne related well to the life of an outcast, or someone who does not do well in school. This book is very well written, though not a book I would choose to read.

This book was not very exciting. It had some high points, but I did not enjoy it. The books I read are exciting and action-packed, whereas this book was not. A book that relates well to me should be fun to read and enjoyable; this book was not. I want to read books about what I have not experienced and probably never will. These books give me a sense of freedom; a sense that maybe I can leave the pressures of my world behind. The book Flour Babies did not give me this experience, but only repeated back to me what I have already experienced.

Anne Fine wrote this story to show people two ideas. One of them is the responsibility of a child and the other is to show what it is like to have a parent walk out on you. This book tells what a person goes through trying to live with one parent, knowing that he had another at one time. Simon, the main character in the book, experiences many emotions over his lost father. He finds that he has avoided the issue for many a year, perhaps a few too many. With the responsibility of a flour baby, Simon first believes that he was too much of a burden to his father, then blames himself for his father's leaving. Simon confronts his mother several times, but the issue of his father is painful for her, and she does not like to talk about it very much. What Simon goes through, being in high school, and not having thought of his father for a long time, is the emotions of the grief process. By the grief process, I mean he first went through denial, then anger. Next he went through grief, and finally acceptance.

This story also illustrates child care. The responsibility of child is a big one. Even though Simon only has to take care of a sack of flour, it is still a difficult task. It made Simon appreciate all that his mom had done for him. It also made him see why his mom sometimes let him sit in a booth by himself and be bored. This book can make people think twice about having a child because after reading it, a person will see everything that Simon had to go through and rethink pregnancy.

This book had special meaning to me because it got me thinking about what has happened to me. Though a father walking out and being put up for adoption are different, in a way they are alike. Flour Babies made me think about what I may be able to do in the ways of finding information about my biological parents. It made me think about why I was put up for adoption, and then like Simon, I really don't care. My biological parents put me up for adoption a long time ago. It was for a good reason I'm sure, but they don't matter to me one bit because I was put with a new family, the Youngrens. They are the only family I have ever known, and they are the only ones that matter.

Each support topic creatively examines and connects ideas. A piece which meets the criteria given earlier but is also fresh and intriguing should be rated at the advanced level. Authors at this level begin to see and communicate their subject with a slightly different, maybe even surprising, slant. Perhaps they use different support topics than may be expected, as they strive to see more support than what is obvious or predictable. Or perhaps they use predictable points, but connect them to the thesis differently than may be expected. The author may even include stories or anecdotes that build support in an interesting way, drawing the reader into the argument. Ryan uses this technique in his piece about the A-10 Thunderbolt:

It's a cool spring morning on a large, open plain. The air is clear, the sky is blue, and the birds are chirping. There is a faint rumbling in the background, which is steadily getting louder. Soon, all other noise has ceased, and all that is on the plain is a couple Russian built T-32 main battle tanks, two armoured troop carriers, and a ZSU-28 anti-aircraft tank. They rumble across the plain as if they had not a care in the world.

The lead tank comander is sitting on top of his tank for some fresh air. He thinks he has chosen the best route in which to avoid any confrontation on their way to get resupplied. He hears a faint whine and then suddenly, he hears a great explosion from behind. In terror, he turns to look, and sees an A-10 Thunderbolt has just blown up one of the troop carriers and is closing in on his convoy. He alerts the anti-aircraft tank. The tank turns, but is soon halted by the A-10's main gun. The comander alerts his tank guner to fire the tanks missle at the incoming plane. As the plane flys over the gunner fires the missle. The commander congratulates his crew on the kill. He looks out his hatch only to see that the A-10 has deployed chaffe to fool the missle, and is coming around for another pass. The A-10 targets the tank, and with a short burst of fire from its main gun the tank is obliterated. The A-10 then fires a Maverick air-to-ground missle and destroys the remaining armoured troop carrier.

The plane used in the above is the A-10 Thunderbolt. Also known as the "WARTHOG" or "TANK KILLER." The military is trying to decommission this plane. They say its too slow and combersom, and that it is very vulnerable to AAA (Anti-Aircraft Artillery) and AA (Anti Aircraft) fire. If the military does actually decommission this plane, our spouses, siblings, children, and relatives in the armed forces could be in danger. Without air support they will be sitting ducks for other artillery and tanks. The ground forces rely heavily upon air support to help them. When they have the support they can then do what they were trained to do.

Despite what the military says, the A-10 is actually the perfect plane for the job of close-air-support. The A-10 was designed around the main gun, which has seven barrels, weighs two tons, and can fire 60 to 70 depleted uranium, armour piercing rounds per second, which can turn a tank into swiss cheese in seconds. The engines, which are not conventional jet engines, are turbo fan engines which are similar to what is used on commercial airliners. They use these because jet engines are too fast for air support and can be heard from miles away. The turbo fans are slower and very quiet.

The body of the aircraft is designed to take multiple hits and continue flying (for example, half a wing missing and only one engine left). The tail fins are set apart in order to increase the chance of escaping from heat seeking missles. They dissapate the heat signature making the air less hot. As for the pilot, he is very well protected. He sits, literally, in a bathtub made of titanium steel, which can protect him from shells as large as 23mm. You may be thinking, "So there's a lot of armour and stuff. What about the controls?" Most aircraft have dual hydraulic controls. So if one is shot out the pilot can still use the other one. However, these controls are placed side by side and can be destroyed with a well placed shot. Unlike most other aircraft the A-10's dual controls are set apart. It also has a backup system of cables similar to those used on WWII aircraft. Also, unlike most other aircraft, the fuel tanks aren't in the wings, can reseal themselves when punctured, and cannot be ignited by an incidniary bullet. Right now you might be thinking, "Wow! This sounds like the perfect plane. Are there any drawbacks?" Well, actually, yes there are. Because of the engines that are used, the A-10 doesn't have the power to dogfight with an actual air-to-air fighter aircraft, it loses power and thrust at high altitudes, and is not fast enough to evade them. However the A-10 is equiped with a radar that detect aircraft many miles away, and two air-to-air Sidewinder missles.

As you can see the A-10 was designed to be durable, aggressive and mean. But when the military decides to decommission this plane, your spouses, siblings, children, and relatives won't have the lead spewing, metal twistn', turn tanks into swiss cheese air support they need badly.

However, if we can make the military realize the value of this aircraft our loved ones might not have to worry. All the military has to do is refit the plane with better turbo fans and better radar and electronics. If these upgrades were done the plane would make the war zone a safer place for our loved ones.

We need to gather everyone with a spouse, sibling, child or relative together. We then need to make the military see that this plane means alot to us and our loved ones. We can do this by carrying picket signs in front of military recruers offices, our state senetors and congressmen, the white house, and the military HQ itself, the Pentagon. It may take a while to gather everyone together and coordinate this, but our loved ones are worth it. And the sooner we start the sooner the A-10 will be protecting us once again.

Evidence

Mature authors do more than just argue a point and provide three or more reasons for that point. They include many details that convince readers of the authority of their text. Details may include facts, statistics, quotations, descriptions, anecdotes, and more. Each detail is included with obvious thought behind it—evidence that the author has analyzed the data collected and put it together to gain personal meaning.

Nonassessable

A paper that provides no evidence to substantiate the support topics is nonassessable for evidence. Early content-area writers, especially those who are learning to write a basic paragraph, will state a thesis, give three or more reasons for that thesis, and conclude the piece. This is developmentally acceptable for young writers. Brittany's piece about good leaders is a perfect example:

What does it mean to be a good leader? A good leader is someone who people want to follow. A good leader never gives up. Like in the movie Iron Will, the dog never gave up. He is a real good leader. A good leader is also smart and wise so people want to follow that person.

Emerging

A writer with an emerging grasp of evidence occasionally provides it to substantiate support topics. At this point, the writer has graduated; he or she realizes that something is needed to prove supporting points, that his or her own reasons for believing them are not enough. Even if the amount of evidence is insufficient, a piece that includes some evidence for its argument should be rated as emerging. Whitney, for example, substantiates (though minimally) why she thinks the Incas were good farmers:

Incas were very good farmers. They would put leftover food in the fields. This would help plants grow, just like fertilizer.

Developing Through Advanced

At more mature levels, writers include a sufficient amount of evidence to prove each point. While the word "sufficient" implies some judgment on the rater's part, objectivity may be enhanced by considering this question: Is there enough evidence to substantiate each claim? Perhaps the author has included three pieces of evidence for each support topic. Or perhaps the author has included fewer than three, but made a strong effort to communicate the evidence well or connect it to the argument. Whatever the case, to be rated at these more advanced levels, the support topics cannot be floating on their own; they must be anchored by concrete evidence.

The following are signs of an author's increasing grasp of the use of evidence.

The evidence provided is relevant.   Evidence used to prove a point must relate clearly to the point being proved. Whether the relationship is self-evident or requires establishment by the author, the relevance should be unmistakable.

Dani asserts in her paper that the computer made an impact on society similar to that of the printing press in the Renaissance. Her support topics include typing, data storage, the Internet, the World Wide Web, e-mail, games, and jobs. Each support topic is substantiated by evidence:

The printing press was an incredible invention in the Renaissance time period. It made printing much easier. A similar invention has also made things easier in the twentieth century. This extraordinary invention is the computer. The computer has made life much easier for many people. Already, the computer has progressed a lot. Many improvements and changes have made the computer what it is today.

The computer is a machine which allows a person to type. Unlike the typewriter, the computer allows you to make changes and view your work before it is printed. This is very helpful for many reasons. One reason is because many people make mistakes when they type. The computer allows one to modify these mistakes. With this privilege, one can also rearrange the order in which the document flows. For example, a person is able to switch the location of a paragraph in order to make their document better. Typing on the computer has also revolutionized newspaper companies, just as the printing press did. Now newspaper editors have a much easier time of printing, editing, and shifting the columns of the newspaper.

Computers also store tons of information. The computer can "remember" data that is programmed into it, as well as information that is saved onto its hard drive. The storage of data is very important to businesses. Because of the computer, there is hardly any need for much of the hand filing and hand record keeping that used to be needed.

A recent contribution to the computer world is the Internet. The Internet is very useful to people and businesses that need to communicate with people on the other side of the world. The Internet also helps people tell others things that they need to know. People can get in touch with the Internet through a helpful device called a modem.

One part of the Internet is the World Wide Web. The World Wide Web helps people to receive information. There are many things that are offered on the World Wide Web. One can receive information on almost any subject that one can possibly think of. The World Wide Web also makes available lots of information. Some of the information that you could receive on the World Wide Web is: weather, news, comedy, advertising, and sports scores.

When a person needs information about a topic, they can just get on the World Wide Web. Then they can ask the computer to look up their topic. This is done by typing a subject into the computer and then clicking the mouse on "search." The computer will then transfer this "search request" to another computer through a modem. Another computer, believe it or not, will send the requested information back to the person's computer. The person can then look at the list of documents, web-sites, about or related to their topic. Thus allowing the consumer to get the information that they need.

Another useful part of the Internet is e-mail. E-mail is incredibly helpful for communication to other people. Many people use e-mail to keep in touch with their friends. Others use it to announce upcoming or past events. E-mail is used by many because of its speed. People also use the e-mail as opposed to letters because of its efficiency. Using e-mail has a very low cost. These are some of the reasons that people use e-mail for communication. The e-mail is a very important part of the Internet. The Internet is only accessed through a computer. Consequently, a computer is very important for getting information and knowledge.

Computers also offer games that can be loaded on to them. These games help improve skills and knowledge. Some academic skill areas which have games for the computer include math, social studies, and literature. This can be very helpful to teach and improve skills.

The field of computers is very elaborate and complex. There are many jobs in the field of computers. There are the designers, the constructors, the "change-makers," and the consumers. These are all very significant jobs. Another job that couldn't be forgotten is the job of the people who fix computers when they break. The computer repair person is very important. The people who work in the field of computers or work with computers are smart. Technology is a hard thing to keep up with, and these people seem to do it well.

With technology changing so rapidly, the competition among computer manufacturers is also growing. This makes the computers that we use better. This is because the manufacturers compete with each other to come out with a better product. The computer is such a wonderful machine that does so much in so many ways. This makes the computer among the best of the inventions that have been invented in the twentieth century.

The evidence provided is documented.   How the evidence is documented depends on the assigned format for the piece, but if evidence is collected from outside sources, they should be credited. For younger authors, this may mean a simple indication of who said what ("Julie said . . .") or what general source was used ("According to the movie we saw . . ."). For more experienced authors, especially if a format is assigned, the citing of sources involves bibliographies, footnotes, and/or in-context quotes and references.

The evidence provided is varied.   Evidence that comes from only one source is automatically assumed to be biased in favor of the person writing the report. Again, the number three becomes key, since using only two sources can result in an argument that is flat and thin. Including at least one more source "shapes up" the argument so it can withstand scrutiny.

But variety means more than just number of sources. It also means number of *types* of sources. If the three sources used are all books written at the same time or by the same person or group, they may fail to be convincing. When considering variety, a rater should check for varied authors, varied copyright dates, and varied formats (books, magazines, journals, software, the Internet, interviews, experiences, audio-visual materials, and so forth).

Rachel's paper on the poison dart frog, for example, includes evidence from a biology textbook, a trade book on poisonous animals, a nature magazine, and a zoology text. All are listed in her bibliography, and she weaves the information together to create support for each assertion in her paper:

There are more than forty members of the Poison Dart Frog family. The levels of classification for the Phyllobates terribilis are:

Phylum: Chrodata
Sub-Phylum: Vertebrata
Class: Amphibia
Family: Rahinae
Genus: Phyllobates
Species: Terribilis

The Phyllobates Terribilis is found in the tropical rain forests of South America, throughout Brazil and Colombia.

Adaptive features of phyllobates terribilis are its bright, colorful skin that is a warning to predators, its poison to defend itself and its suction cup feet which aid it to climb trees in the forest.

Their behavioral patterns include defensive, reproductive and parenting. For defense, they have poison in their skin. They usually taste really bad, and an unlucky predator like a bird will drop it in a hurry. The animal probably won't die from their experience, but they won't try to eat any brightly colored prey in the future.

Frogs reproduce sexually. Male frogs make a chirping sound to his mate to persuade her to lay eggs. The female then will release as many as six eggs, then the male fertilizes them. Poison dart frogs lay their eggs in a leaf canopy. After the tadpoles hatch, the male carries them on his back until he finds a safe puddle.

Native South Americans use the frogs by dipping the tips of their darts in a potion made from the frog's poison. After they have shot an animal with their dart from a blow gun, they will follow the darted animal around the forest until it collapses and dies. This frog's poison causes irreversible muscle contractions that lead to heart failure.

Some poison dart frogs have a poison 200 times the strength of morphine. That is now being researched as a medication for patients who don't respond to pain medication now.

The evidence provided is valid and reliable. Evidence that is *valid* does just what it sets out to do: prove the point for which it was selected. If the evidence used is incorrect or outdated, how can it prove the point? When checking evidence for validity, raters look for information that is specific, accurate, and current.

Evidence that is *reliable* is evidence that can be used by several different people, who will likely find that it leads them to the same conclusion. When checking for reliability, raters look for evidence that is unbiased and that comes mostly from accepted authorities on the topic. Propaganda from political organizations and information from tourism boards are examples of biased evidence, which may be used but must be balanced with evidence from sources that have less to gain by persuading audiences to move in a certain direction.

Here are some examples that illustrate validity and reliability:

- Evidence from a book on space published in the 1960s would be too outdated (and therefore invalid) to substantiate an argument about life on Mars, though it might well be appropriate for *part* of an argument on the *history* of space travel.
- Quoting evidence from a 1960s book on Bob Dylan would be wholly appropriate, but using only books from the 1960s by the same author would be biased and therefore unreliable.
- For a persuasive paper on why chewing gum should be allowed in class, only interviewing students would render the evidence both invalid (students don't know the whole story), and unreliable (it would be important to interview an accepted authority on the messes made by chewing gum, such as a custodian or a health authority).
- Any piece that includes only evidence taken from the Internet or an encyclopedia contains invalid evidence (an encyclopedia is too general, and material on the Internet is not subject to copyright or checks for accuracy).

In Savanna's speech supporting the school bond election in her school district, no bibliography was assigned. Still, she documented her evidence, which she gleaned from newspaper articles and school board reports. She avoided propaganda from the local teachers' union and even parent organizations. Selecting reliable evidence lent credibility to her argument that a new high school would soon be needed to prevent overcrowding:

> **Hi. I'm Savanna Beaver, as you already know. The bond issue talks about how much we need or don't need a new high school so we will not have**

as much crowding in the schools. I believe that you should vote for the bond issue because school enrollment is going up across the nation. School enrollment is UP a lot in District six.

This year an estimated 51.7 million students head to school, more than any other time in the history of the U.S. The Education Department says that U.S. school enrollment is going to rise to 54.6 million by the year 2006. Some will surely see this increase of students as a liability, but in the long run, they are a tremendous asset to our nation—if we teach them well. Education Secretary Richard Rilley said, "to meet the demand, an estimated 190,000 more teachers and more than 6,000 schools will be needed." As our nation grows, so does district six enrollment.

Cameron Elementary school is above what it can hold right now, but lots more schools are expected to go above what they can hold soon. Two schools—Centennial and Dos Rios—are right at their base line because the extra kids are being sent to other schools. It is the 11th straight year that the number of kids has grown in the district, putting more students in classes, making teachers work in packed rooms, and making halls too crowded for students to navigate and still get to classes on time.

At the beginning of the year Greeley Central High School was 8 students away from what the school can hold, and Greeley West High School was 78 students away from what the school can hold. According to last year's numbers, enrollment has grown 26% or 2,906 students since 1985. According to the Education Secretary, "Public high schools will enroll 15% more students in the next 10 years."

And now I hope that you understand why we should vote for more schools and more teachers.

We live in the Information Age. Even the development of voice-activated computers will not keep future generations from needing the ability to compose expository pieces. Their importance is suggested by the fact that they are assigned in almost every class, especially in the later grades. Practice does not make perfect, however, though it may make habits permanent. Good expository writing entails a variety of specific skills that can be taught and measured. Why not teach and evaluate expository skills and strategies that *should* become permanent?

ASSESSING
LANGUAGE,
STYLE, AND
MECHANICS IN
ANY PIECE

four

oth narrative and expository writing involves using elements of language and style (sentence structure, paragraph development, and voice) and mechanics (punctuation, capitalization, and spelling). This chapter explains how to assess these elements in both types of writing.

Sentence Structure

he purpose of writing is to express ideas. Narrative writing uses ideas to tell a story, while expository writing uses ideas to build and support an argument. A mature author communicates ideas in complete thoughts that the reader can read and understand smoothly and easily.

Nonassessable

If the ideas in a piece of writing are decipherable only by the author, the sentence structure is nonassessable. Very young authors draw pictures or "write" strings of letters or shapes that have meaning only to them. When asked, however, they are sometimes able to read their pieces aloud. When they do so, listeners can tell that the writing of these young

Figure 4.1 Miranda's Thank-You Note

authors does have meaning. Students at this stage of development should be rated nonassessable for sentence structure (writers who cannot decipher their own pieces are not ready to have their pieces assessed using the Author's Profile). If their teachers encourage daily writing, read aloud, and in general provide a literate environment, young writers soon decipher their own work and move on to more advanced stages. Miranda's thank-you note is an example of work decipherable only by the author (see Figure 4.1).

Emerging

Writing that displays an emerging level of sentence structure contains ideas that are written in words, phrases, run-on sentences, or incomplete sentences that are decipherable. Many developing authors skip this stage, since most tend to write just as they talk. Some, however, hear the sentences in their heads and skip important words or phrases while struggling to get their ideas on paper. Others, especially second language learners, struggle with how the English language is structured. The result is a piece that is understandable but is plagued with sentence fragments, as in Andy's piece:

A chita looking for its pray. A lion kat its pray and it is about to eat it. Tow laprds. One is jumping to a zebra. Hear is some girafs. Tow laprd's fiting on a big roke.

(A cheetah looking for its prey. A lion caught its pray, and it is about to eat it. Two leopards. One is jumping to a zebra. Here is some giraffes. Two leopards fighting on a big rock.)

Developing Through Advanced

Sentence structure is more than a measure of correctness. Even young authors can construct simple subject-verb sentences that are flawless. As writers mature, however, they tend to add variety and length to their sentences. They also occasionally combine sentences or change their structure to avoid sounding repetitive. Each level of growth adds a new dimension of correctness, a new editing challenge.

Remember: *sentence structure, capitalization, and punctuation are all separate issues.* When rating for sentence structure, look for complete thoughts and appropriate joining of words and phrases, not for correct capitalization and punctuation. A good rule of thumb to follow when considering sentence structure is to consider what the piece sounds like when read aloud. If it makes sense and follows the appropriate conventions for speaking, chances are the sentence structure is reasonably well developed.

The following are indications of developing sentence structure.

In general, sentences are correctly structured. At the developing level, subject and predicate are correctly used in simple sentences. Sentences that are complete contain both a subject and a predicate. Also check for agreement between subject and verb ("She has" vs. "She have"), noun and pronoun ("Every boy to himself" vs. "Every boy to themselves"), verb and adverb ("walk slowly" vs. "walk slow"). In the following story of Ben's, his sentences are flawlessly structured:

This is me at the train station. I was going to my grandma and grandpa's house in Illinois. I slept the night on the train. I wok up. I aot bracfit. It wos gud. I brosht my teeth. I made my bad . . .

(This is me at the train station. I was going to my grandma and grandpa's house in Illinois. I slept the night on the train. I woke up. I ate breakfast. It was good. I brushed my teeth. I made my bed . . .)

In general, sentences begin in a variety of ways.   Once authors feel comfortable building sentences, they begin to want more variety in their sentences. The easiest way to gain variety is to change the way sentences begin. Connor, while maintaining simple sentences, tries out this technique:

> **Hi my name is Ben. I'm in London. They have put in baseball as a sport. They're taking down a castle for a field. We have the shields. I'm going to the game tomorrow. It will be fun to see them play for the first time . . .**

Leo's expository piece also illustrates sentences that begin differently:

> **My favorite hobby is dancing for the "Greeley Rodarte Dancers." They are a Mexican folk dance group. The dance group has existed for 5 years. They have danced in Colorado, Wyoming and Texas. We recently attended a national dance competition in Lubbock, Texas . . .**

In general, sentences vary in length.   When read aloud, stories tend to exhibit a certain rhythm. In some pieces, as in Connor's story above, the rhythm is similar, almost repetitive, throughout. In other pieces, the repetition is broken by using sentences of different lengths, even if they remain simple in structure. Haley takes advantage of this variety:

> **Have you ever felt sand so hot it burned your feet? We went to the sand dunes on our vacation. We had fun.**
> **We made dams so the water would stay there. We got dirty. It was fun. Then we slid down the dunes. It was fun.**
> **I got sand in my pants. We had to wash it out. My feet got burned on the hot sand when we climbed up the dunes. We used our hands and feet. We stuck our feet down in the sand to cool them off. We had fun.**

Joe, like Leo, wrote a piece about his hobby. His sentences have a little more variety in length. He includes some compound sentences, but no complex sentences yet:

> **My favorite hobby is drawing. I've done so much stuff with it, I don't even know how to explain it! First when I was a little kid about 3 years old is**

when I started to draw. When I got up to 7 years old, I started shading things in. Then when I turned 10 years old, I went to a professional drawing class in Denver Colorado. I got 2nd out of all 1,050 kids that went. I went back to Greeley and right when I came in the door my mom was so happy for me she was practically crying! She put my poster in a frame. It made me happy! . . .

In general, sentences include compound and complex forms. As writers become more experienced, their use of language develops. They move away from simple thoughts towards more complex ones. To express themselves, they necessarily move from simple sentences to more complex sentences. They begin to combine complete thoughts, draw connections, and insert more ideas in their sentences. Breann's piece shows she is beginning to combine sentences for smoother, less choppy reading:

Jennifer, who is eight years old and has silky black hair down just past her shoulders, opened a tiny present. It was wrapped in very soft wrapping paper with a cute little string tied around it. After untying the string and carefully unwrapping the paper she took off the lid on the box . . .

Luke's piece of expository writing (part of which was seen in Chapter 3) includes both complex and compound sentences. Even though his punctuation needs work, reading the piece aloud reveals a mature sentence structure. Those sentences that remain fragments, if added to the sentences that precede or follow, would add complexity to the sentences. When this piece is read aloud, unnecessary punctuation tends to go away, lending general correctness to the piece.

One August morning in 1977, history, tales, and legends would be changed. The second of its kind, was scheduled to go before it's twin. For 176 years they have been waiting. Only now can it be successful in it's purpose in life. The name given to both is very appropriate, for they go farther than the human mind can imagin. Powered by the longest lasting, most powerful force known to man, the twins travel on a highway of discovery on plutonium. Not only designed for discovery <u>for</u> humans, but designed for discovery <u>of</u> humans. This pair, of course, is Voyager I and II.

Voyager II was launched August 20, 1977. It's twin September 5, of the same year. Although number one was the latter, it went off a faster trajectory and lead the way. The result of going faster was not as good of pictures. Unlike Voyager II, number two went slower and took better pictures and collected better information than his twin. The two orbited each outer planet for awhile then used the planet's momentum to throw itself to another planet. They only were together for colossal Jupiter and beautiful

Saturn. After Saturn, they split up. Voyager I used the momentum of Saturn's gravitational pull and projected itself out of our solar system. Saturn was number one's last picture show for it's expedition. But his twin's job was yet unfinished. Number two, after Saturn, did Uranus and Neptune, skipping the dainty Pluto. Neptune being the last stop because it is the farthest. Pluto will be inside Neptune's orbit until 1999. When Voyager II is done with our solar system, it will shut everything down except for some sensors. If the sensors pick up life forms or anything important, the whole system boots up and relays messages to earth. This process will continue until the plutonium runs out. A little box on the outer skeleton contains a map to earth and descriptions of humans. This may work to our disadvantage, but it was a gamble necessary to discover the long asked question. This is for anybody who finds this beat-up piece of junk.

The reason I chose this as a major invention was because it gave us so much. We know now that Saturn isn't the only planet with rings. Jupiter, Uranus and Neptune all have rings as well. We found out temperatures, mass, diameter, and exactly how far away the planets are. Voyager identified moons we couldn't have seen otherwise. They gave us visual and mathematical descriptions of alien surfaces. The Voyagers may even discover new life. Voyagers may even discover us.

Paragraph Development

Paragraphs prevent readers from having, on their own, to sort out dialogue between characters (Who's saying what?) and to organize events (Did we switch subjects?). Well-written paragraphs create and maintain a focus on one event, description, or character, allowing the reader to sit back and enjoy the writing knowing they won't get lost in the story or the report.

Nonassessable

If a piece is presented as a set of seemingly disconnected or randomly ordered ideas, the piece should not be rated for paragraph development. Brian's story from Chapter 2 comes to mind again here:

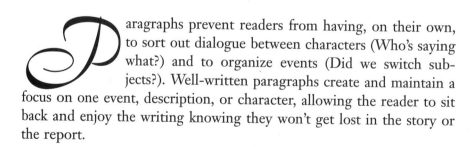

The fish was bedt by sbmaes. The safr was no the taop. The big samaben came and it was explring. The big samaren was going fastr. Tine a big big samaren came. A bote hit a isbrg. And it sild oill.

(The fish was protected by submarines. The surfer was on the top. The big submarine came, and it was exploring. The big submarine was going faster. Then a big, big submarine came. A boat hit an iceberg. And it spilled oil.)

Emerging

A piece containing an emerging level of paragraph development contains ideas that are logically ordered. There are several logical ways to put ideas in order. The most obvious is chronological, where events that take place first are listed first and events that happen later are positioned later. Authors may also choose to order ideas based on common themes, such as happy memories and unhappy memories. Others may choose to order events by the character involved in each one. Still others may want to show cause and effect—what happened, and then why it happened.

Leo's piece, mentioned earlier in this chapter, is an example of a young writer's sense of order. His ideas are well ordered as he works through a description of his hobby, but there is no paragraphing.

> My favorite hobby is dancing for the "Greeley Rodarte Dancers." They are a Mexican folk dance group. The dance group has existed for 5 years. They have danced in Colorado, Wyoming and Texas. We recently attended a national dance competition in Lubbock, Texas. I won two medals and one trophy for best male dancer 12–16. The group also brought home four medals and two trophys. I like to dance because it gives me something to do. I get to meet new people, make friends and learn about my culture. I learn about my ancestors. I like to think that I am carrying on the tradition. When the Greeley Rodarte dancers perform sometimes I get nervous. Even though I've been dancing for 7 years. When I get up on stage, I see the hundreds of eyes staring at me. I worry about falling or messing up. When I hear my fellow dancers yell gretos (Spanish cheers) I feel comfortable. I feel at home. When I am done dancing I have to change my costume. Sometimes I don't have a lot of time so I hurry. I run to the dressing room and change my clothes. After a performance, sometimes we eat. My friends and I talk about dancing. What we did bad and what we could do to improve. Soon its time for us to leave when I get home, I think about the next performance. I wait for the day to come again.

Developing Through Advanced

In more advanced levels of paragraph development, expectations for the organization of ideas increase. Not only are ideas ordered, but they are separated into paragraphs. The most mature paragraphs are indented, begin anew for each idea or speaker, have topic sentences with supporting details where appropriate, and progress smoothly from one to the next.

Ideas are separated into groups.   Once authors logically order their ideas, they begin to find ways to separate them into groups. At the developing level, they look for ways to show the reader that the story or information is moving on. For example, whenever a young author arrives at a new idea, he or she may draw a picture to separate the new idea from the one before it, or start a whole new page, or perhaps skip a line.

Curt's report is divided by pages. He carefully organized his ideas into groups and then wrote each on a separate sheet of paper. No indents are evident.

> **[Page 1]**
> This report is about the Planet Jupiter. Jupiter is a giant planet. Larger and heavier than all the other planets combined.
>
> **[Page 2]**
> You can see Jupiter's sixteen moons through a small telescope. Stell Jupiter has at least 16 moons. One of Jupiter's moons is called the Pizza moon. Also with Jupiter's 16 moons there is a reing.
>
> **[Page 3]**
> If Jupiter were hollo, more then 1,400 planet Earths could fit inside. No one has seen what Jupiter is like beneath it's clouds. Jupiter's year is 4380 days. Next to Jupiter the other planets shrink.
>
> **[Page 4]**
> The red spot seems to be a long lasting storm. The scientists have watched the red spot for more then 200 years the scientists think the red spot is a storm and gases.
>
> **[Page 5]**
> I hoped you liked my report. it would be fun to fly passed Jupiter and see it's many moon, rings, and spot. It would take many Earth years but even less Jupiter years to get there.

Paragraphs are indented.   At the practicing level, young authors learn that the accepted way to separate ideas is into paragraphs. They begin to indent every once in a while, sometimes when they feel they need a space on the paper, and other times when they have switched to a new idea or event. Jamie, for example, knew she needed some separations in her piece on volleyball. Some of her paragraphs, however, actually contain more than one topic:

> I started playing volleyball when my brother started to play with my sister-in-law. I was about in the 6th grade when I started to play with Scott (my brother) and Connie (my sister-in-law).
>
> We could start playing in 7th grade and I knew I whated to play for my school. At first I did not get along with my coach but after a while we just got along. I could not play that well so I went to a volleyball camp at my

school. You have to get your servers in to get a point, and I was very bad at serving. My borther said he would help me on my serves. I started playing for the Recratichion Center.

I played my first game in April and we won are first game. We always practice on Tuesdays and Thursdays. I like most of the people on my team. Most of the time my coach is nice. Her name is Jenn. We played four games. We won are first three games. Our last game we lost. So we were three and one (volleyball talk.) Then we played may 3rd and almost all of my family was there.

We were 3rd in terenaments and we were going to play 4th in the terenaments but we played the 1st in the terenaments. We lost that game. So we will play may 17th. I think my brother is going to come this time. We are playing in terenaments again.

I like this game so much because I look up to my brother and because I just love this game so much. I like that I can get so much help from my brother and sister-in-law. I know that I will play volleyball anytime and any where because I love it so much.

Paragraphs begin with each new idea or speaker.   Also at the practicing stage, authors have finally made the transition to using paragraphs as signals for their readers. They recognize that paragraphs are used when they change subjects, switch to a new event or time, or allow a new character to speak. They also understand that first lines of new paragraphs are indented. Clay recognizes the need for paragraphs and indents in his piece on boats of the Mississippi. Many times, however, he is off on a new paragraph before developing the last one.

The Mississippi is like a highway to the people who use it. On it you will find many types of boats, barges and ships.

Barges carry many products. They can carry grain, petroleum, coal, vegetable oil, sulphur, and machinery.

A full tow of 16 barges is the size of 3 football fields!

A different type of cargo ship on the Mississippi is called a Freighter. Freighters carry solid cargo and tankers carry liquid cargo.

Many freighters leave the Mississippi and carry cargo to another country.

If a cargo ship carries only bananas, it is called a banana ship.

Towboat's engines are usually not shut off for 8 months or more.

Boats carry more than just cargo, they carry many people on the Mississippi. Riverboats with paddle wheels on the back are a popular way to travel . . .

Where appropriate, paragraphs have topic sentences and supporting details.   A topic sentence in a paragraph signals for the reader what the new subject, event, time, or character will be. In general, paragraphs often should contain a topic sentence that gives the main idea of the paragraph. Every subsequent sentence in the paragraph should maintain focus on that topic, not stray to a different idea. Ben's book report illustrates paragraphs that are well developed:

Even though the students in room 8 (the slackers, underachievers, and low grade students) may not have witnessed Simon's promise, Simon Martin got his "glorious explosion." Over 100 lbs of sifted white flour had been kicked, torn, or thrown as far as the eye could see in a corridor of the St. Boniface School. The flour had come from burlap bags, representing babies in a Room 8 child development experiment. The boys had been instructed to look after and take around the five pound "flour baby" . . .

As soon as I opened the book, Flour Babies, I was hooked. The author is a wonderful writer, and has worked the English language in amazing ways. The description and wording of the book was outstanding. The themes in the book were very complex, and all were brought on by five pound sacks of flour. In particular, I especially enjoyed the personification of Simon's "flour baby," Simon's thoughts and emotions, and the novel's twist about the opposites Martin Simon and Simon Martin. My only disappointment was Mr. Cassidy's negativity, but I can certainly see where he is coming from. Furthermore, the book also contained a good lesson to be learned: don't get into parenting until you are sure you are ready to take on all the responsibilities.

Whenever I come across "writer's block," often given to me is the advice, "Write what you know about." If this applied to the author, Anne Fine, maybe she had someone close to her leave. Writers often use personal experiences to write about, and also write to help them cope with the issue at hand. Perhaps when Simon concluded that, "He's (his dad) really nothing at all to do with me. And out there in the world there are millions and millions of people who have nothing to do with me, who don't even know me. They all get on perfectly well without me. And I do perfectly well without them." This was not only a perfect ending to the book, but also may have been a satisfactory ending to the mystery of an unknown family member. Of course, the idea may have just been conjured by a teen in the mall with a sack of flour. Who knows?

Although I enjoyed this book a lot, it was not that meaningful to me. I have never even thought about fathering a child, yet. The book however may have just supported the fact that I am definitely not ready to have a child, and won't be for quite a long while. It may also not have appealed to me because I have not carried around a baby, but eighth grade is rolling around. Regardless of all this, I enjoyed the book immensely and will always remember loving it.

Occasionally, a break between paragraphs is used simply to indicate a change in speakers. In this case, a topic sentence is not necessary, but it must be clear who is speaking, and the remaining sentences in the paragraph must be focused on what the same character says or does. Katie's story contains many paragraphs that contain only one sentence of dialogue:

> A couple days after Halloween, the curious five year old girl on the block wandered if people at school would think she had big feet if she wore the boots she had gotten from her sister's friend. Nobody was watching her, she snuck in her room and pulled out the ugliest pair of gray boots. She put them on and started trooping around the house like a marine. "Katie ware are you? I've got a present." How bad Katie wanted that present, but she had to hide. Mom didn't want her wearing those boots.
>
> "I know where you are"
>
> "Awe man" katie shouted out.
>
> "yes it works. Are you wearing those boots I told you not to?"
>
> "No . . ." Katie quickly took off the boots and shoved them behind her.
>
> "Well its time for dinner. Go wash up."
>
> "Okay" that night they were having spaghetti for dinner. "yes I can gross my sister out." Katie sat down and just about grabbed her fork then picked up a noodle and sucked it up. "ssssssssp"
>
> "Eeeewww!" screamed Meghan. "Mom Katie did again!" . . .

Paragraphs move smoothly from one to another.　In a well-written piece, paragraph divisions serve as road signs to the reader that the topic is changing, but the change is not abrupt or disconnected from what came before. Transition sentences smooth the road, gently moving the piece from one idea to the next and showing the reader connections between ideas. Whether transitions occur at the end of one paragraph or the beginning of the next, the journey from one to another should be smooth and seamless. Matt, in his piece about the Lynx Black Cat irons reproduced in Chapter 3, has seamless transitions between his support topics (each of which happens to be a paragraph). Erika provides transitions between her paragraphs as well, although with less finesse. Her piece is an analysis of a Langston Hughes poem:

> "Life for me ain't been no crystal stair." In Langston Hughes poem, "Mother to Son," the mother is speaking generally to her son about trials of life, hers in particular. At the beginning of this poem, the mother is preparing her son for what she is going to share with him when she says her life hasn't been a "crystal stair." Langston Hughes describes the mother

examining her own life, the mother telling her son not to become discouraged, and the mother not becoming discouraged herself.

First, the mother examines her own life. She speaks of splinters, tacks, torn up boards, and bare floors on the stairs of her life. When she says that she's reached "landin's," turned "corners," and sometimes been in the dark, it is evident that her life has been full of different and difficult experiences. When saying that she had reached landings on the stairs, it made sense that sometimes in life, you reach a plateau. Nothing is going wrong; however, everything is familiar. The "corners" that she spoke of are the changes that were made in her life. Directly following the line about turning corners, the mother shares that sometimes she would be in the dark. After you have made a significant change in your life, it may seem a bit "dark" or lonely.

Second, the mother tells her son not to become discouraged. Although this part of the poem is short, it is powerful because a parent's encouragement is often times all that you need to keep going when things get tough. The mother tells her son not to "turn back" or "set down on the steps." This is significant because if you just sit down, then you will not longer be climbing. If you aren't constantly climbing, then life will pass you by.

Last, the mother does not become discouraged herself. "I'se still climbin'." It is important for the son to hear his mother say this becuase he will know that everyone has hard times. This is also important because she says to her son, "don't fall now." There is always something to be encouraged about in every situation.

This advice that the mother passes on to her son is valuable to everybody. It is important to keep climbing no matter how hard life becomes.

Voice

good piece, read aloud, sounds a lot like a lively conversation. It is clear that the ideas are those of the author, and that the words in the piece are purposely selected and are communicated clearly, vividly, and in a distinctly personal way.

Voice is probably the most difficult skill to assess in a piece. Many raters will try to avoid assessing voice because, they say, "It's a personal thing. How can I judge an author's personal style?" However, if voice cannot be assessed, then how can it be taught? Readers judge an author's voice constantly while they're reading, even if they don't label it as such.

Fortunately, there are aspects of voice that can and should be taught and assessed. The most basic of these aspects is originality: Did the author write this piece him- or herself, or is much of it reproduced from another source? While retelling a story in one's own words or paraphrasing research material may sometimes be appropriate, no author should copy materials word for word without acknowledging the source.

Selecting appropriate language for the purpose of a piece can also be taught. Would you want to read a comedy that was written with dull and lifeless language? Would you want to read a research paper that was written in slang, or a dialogue between two teens written in formal English?

In assessing voice, also look for specificity, clarity, and personality in the language.

Nonassessable

In a piece of writing where the wording seems to mimic outside sources, the quality of voice is nonassessable. This level of development describes the young child who is just beginning to understand that writing communicates thought. An example of this stage is a young girl who has a favorite book that she reads again and again; when asked to write a story of her own, she gets her book and copies it down (or she retells it from memory). She proudly illustrates and shares it. This level is wholly appropriate for a young child and should not be judged as wrong or lacking—it's simply that the voice is nonassessable. Bianca's story of Jenny and the green ribbon, given in Chapter 2, is an example of this situation. Another is Savanna's early story, in which she adapts a patterned book of a nursery rhyme to make it her own:

> **Hickory Dickory dock.**
> **The mouse ran up the clock.**
> **The clock struck one, he shot a gun.**
> **Hickory Dickory Dock.**
> **The clock struck two, he played with glue.**
> **The clock struck three, he hurt his knee.**
> **The clock struck four, he asked for more.**
> **The clock struck five, he found a hive . . .**

Voice is also nonassessable when the writer of a research paper looks up the topic in the encyclopedia and copies the article word for word. Such copying may be difficult to determine and may sometimes be falsely assumed. However, if the piece is full of adult, formal-sounding language and the writer cannot fully explain what it means, readers may be safe to assume it has been copied. A personal relationship between teacher and child is helpful here, in both detecting the copying and discussing it with the student. Curt's teacher "red-flagged" his piece; rather than sounding like a child who has learned about wolves, his piece sounds like an encyclopedia entry:

> The wolf is a meat eating animal related to the jackal and the domestic dog. Two main species of wolves are recognized: the gray, or timber, wolf and the red wolf, which now occurs in Texas and the southeastern U.S.
>
> An adult timber wolf measures up to 6 1/2 feet in length, including the tail. The animal may weigh up to 175 pounds. The timber wolf is red-yellow or yellow-gray, with black patches above and white below. Those in the far north may be pure white, and black or brown timber wolves also occur.
>
> The red wolf is somewhat smaller in size and usually darker in color. All wolves are characterized by powerful teeth, bushy tails, and round pupils, and they are distinguished from domestic dogs by certain characteristics of the skull . . .

Emerging

In a piece containing an emerging voice, ideas seem to be expressed in the author's own words. At this point, the author's words sound original. This is not to say that the ideas in the piece are creative, unique, or different, or even that they are appropriate for the subject selected, but simply that the words in the piece are probably not copied from another source. John, for example, writes an illustrated book about the sea:

Thes is a map of the sea.	*(This is a map of the sea.*
A sea otter.	*A sea otter.*
The blooawil is aeting kril	*The blue whale is eating krill.*
Thir ore five maml's and three shorks	*There are five mammals and three sharks.*
This is big blue	*This is a big blue.*
A sea otrre is going too eat sea erchit	*A sea otter is going to eat sea urchins.*
This is a orka	*This is an orca.)*

Miranda's narrative piece, which was dictated after she drew illustrations, is a similar example:

> Friends are looking at a tree. The wind is blowing our hair up. Leah and Sarah are in the windows. We are going on a trip to Cheyenne. We're singing outside. I'm changing my brother's diaper . . .

Developing Through Advanced

At more mature stages, the author communicates with his or her own words, but there is obviously more care given to the selection of those words than is shown at the emerging level. A rater should look for appropriate language that is specific and clear, shows rather than tells, and is distinctly personal. The pages that follow detail these qualities.

The language used is appropriate for the piece. The language the student selects should be appropriate for the piece being written. In a narrative, the language should fit the general mood of the story, whether that mood is sad or comic, light-hearted, satiric, or whatever. The author's point of view should be clear from the language used. Whether the story is being told by a character in the story using the first person (I) or by an unseen narrator in the third person (he/she) the point of view should remain consistent throughout the story.

Michael's story is about a boat race. It is clear that the words selected are his, and that Michael himself (a spectator in the race) is the narrator. He chooses language appropriate for the piece—a simple reporting of an event:

I wat to a bot ras it was cool! I like it thar was a oraj bot and a gren bot I lik the bren bot

(I went to a boat race. It was cool! I like it. There was an orange boat and a green boat. I like the green boat.)

In an expository piece, the criteria is similar: the language should be appropriate for the piece and fairly consistent throughout. Lab reports, for example, use different language than persuasive essays, which use different language from research papers and newspaper articles, and so on.

Blake's essay is about his favorite sport:

I have many favorite sports. But my favorite sport is hockey. I watch every game on T.V. I really enjoy watching the Avalanche games. There is a lot of excitement as I watch the game. The most exciting parts of hockey are the fights, the goals, and all the action. Thats the best sport for me. When the Colorado Avalanche win it is really exciting, because I know every time they win they get closer, and closer to winning the Stanley Cup. I know the Avalanche can beat Detroit if they stay focused and try hard.

I also like hockey because of the players. The Avalanche have some of the best players in hockey today. All year long the Avalanche have been listed number one. But they have also worked the hardest. This is only the secound year the Avalanch have been around. But I know that they will win a lot more Stanly Cup Championships.

The language used is specific and clear.   Authors at the practicing level select words carefully so they can say exactly what they mean. In assessing a piece, look especially for well-selected verbs and nouns. Do they paint a clear picture of what is happening in the story? Are they well chosen, or are too many words used to get a point across? Also study any dialogue in the piece. Does it add to the piece, or does it make the events less clear? Is there a reasonable amount of dialogue, or does all the talking distract the reader from the action?

Kathrine strives to use language that is specific and clear in her story about Harry, the mountain goat. Notice her use of specific, descriptive words ("plodded" instead of "walked," "horrible" instead of "bad"), which add a distinctive feel to her piece:

> Once upon a time there was a mountain goat named Harry. He was the littlest goat on the slope, and all the other goats teased him. Harry was sad. "I'll never be a hero. They're right." he sobbed. So off he plodded until he was far, far away from the rest of the herd. "I guess I'll lay down here." he sighed. After a while he got lonely. "I'll go back now." he decided. As he went back he saw a horrible sight. It was his mother and she was cornered by a Puma! He rushed to save her! Before he could think he had knocked the mountain lion off the cliff. Now he was a hero!

Patrick writes about soccer in specific terms and in his own voice:

> I am going to talk about soccer. First I am going to tell you about the protective wear. There are two categories: regular players and goalies. The goalies have shin guards to keep from getting kicked in the shin. They have gloves so the ball wouldn't hurt as much when the ball was kicked at them. They also have pads in their uniform. Next are the regular players they just have shin guards.
>
> There are eleven positions on the field (the way I play). There are three positions in defense the right, left, center (sometimes called a stopper), and sweeper. Their jobs are to stop the ball from getting to the goalie. The goalie is the one who stops the ball if shot at. There are three midfielders the right, left, and center. They play offense and defense. That's how they got their name midfield. There are three forwards the right, left, and center (sometimes called the striker). The striker stays even with the last defender of the other team. The wings (left and right) come back on defense but they don't go back too far.
>
> There are many rules in the game of soccer. The goalie is the only one who can use hands. If you use hands and you're not the goalie the other team gets a free kick. If one team kicks the ball out of bounds, the other team throws the ball in. You can't lift your foot when you throw the ball.

There are five parts of a uniform the protective wear, shorts, socks, cleets and the jersee. The regular players all have to look the same. The goalie can wear whatever he wants. Every team has a different kind of uniform.

I started to play soccer when I was four years old. I started soccer playing for rec. I played for them for three years. Then I started to play bootleggers. I played for them for four years and I'm still playing for them.

The language used shows rather than tells. As authors become more proficient, they begin to resist the temptation to tell the reader everything they want to communicate. Rather than saying explicitly, for example, that a character is poor, they *show* it in what the character wears, eats, or owns, or in how and where the character lives. Rather than stating that two cars collided, a mature author may show it by describing the loud crash, the debris in the road, the sirens of emergency vehicles, and so on. Clay uses this technique in his story, where he shows through the characters' actions how they react when spotting a tornado. He never says they are afraid, but he manages to convey their emotions through their actions:

We dropped our poles and raced to the car. My dad started the car, and we peeled out.

Erik chooses to show, rather than tell, what medieval apprenticeships were like by creating his narrative in the form of a journal:

I've always known I'd be a carpenter. Ever since I was a little boy, my father and mother have told me how good I am at working with wood. I worked with my father often, during my childhood, and he told me that I had a good eye for measuring. I suppose my previous days have been the culmination to this cold day, or so my elders would have me believe.

I've been riding for four days, in this horrid weather. My clothes were waterlogged in an hour after I left my village, and I think I've taken ill. My life awaits me up ahead through the rain.

The city where I am to be an apprentice is big! Past the gates I ride now, into this hubbub of society. I've been stopped by the guards twice now, but I showed them my letter, and they pointed me in the right direction. It is all so confusing, and so different.

It is a new life for me now. My master was expecting me, when I rode to his place, and a boy was there to take my horse to the stables. The master beckoned me, and told me he wanted to talk to me. I am quite in awe of him. "Welcome to my workshop," he says, and nothing more. I am speechless. He showed me to my quarters, and gave me a meal. He then bade me have a good night, and to sleep well.

I wake up this morning by the hands of another apprentice—and not a gentle one, either. He told me that I was to see the master, and he will begin his teaching. I rose, dressed, and ate, and I went to the master. He told me that he must know what I could do, and told me to make him a chair, of all things, of the finest quality I could. I toiled into the night, making that chair for the master, and when I was finished, the master was pleased. He told me it was a well-made chair, and taught me a few things about how to improve such a chair. I was proud when I went to bed that night.

I must be here, in the master's workshop, because of work like I did that night—I am able, and can make good things, so it must be my fate to be a carpenter. I am glad that the master was pleased with me. He talked to me with praising words about my work. He is a good man, and I am glad to be his apprentice.

I rose again this rosy dawn and broke my fast in lieu of seeing the master. Today, he said, he would show everyone the proper way to shape wood into a thing of beauty. I am alone at this moment, for I don't know what to do, and I feel a fool. The master tells me the way of his shop, and I quickly bend to my task. When all were finished with their pieces of work, the master eyed them all and made remarks about their quality. A couple of the boys cursed at the master under their breath. He flogged them for that. He was right, doing so. Some boys need to learn respect. I'm glad I already know it.

I enjoy woodworking, and I do it well. I've been spared floggings and lectures because I always do what I am told. Under the master's guidance, I hope that I'll be a great carpenter one day, like him. Maybe I'll be the king's carpenter, some time. I dearly hope it will be so.

The days continue to pass in this city, in this workshop, and with each passing day I know more than I did before. I've angered the master once now, but he spared me a flogging. He is a good man, not at all like my brother's master.

I'm learning more from the master every day now. I hope and pray that my conviction to the carpenter's life holds strong. If it should waver, I don't know what I would do. I will see, in the years to come, these long, long years to come. I'll be the master some time.

Erin attempts to show how Emily Dickinson was introverted, how she was often alone with her words even in a crowd:

> . . . When her father would have meetings at the house, Emily would hide in the corner and listen in on their conversations. If she had some-

thing to add, she would write it on a piece of paper and send it to the person she was directing her comment towards.

Wherever she was, whatever she was doing, Emily would pick up a piece of scrap paper and scribble a poem on it if she was inspired to do so. She stuffed the little pieces of paper into drawers, under cushions, behind furniture, into pockets—anywhere she could find within her house. These papers were found by one of her sisters after her death . . .

The language used is distinctly personal. While many aspects of writing can be taught and learned, an advanced level of voice must be found (or perhaps rediscovered). When young authors are not hindered by conventions and rules, they often write with a voice all their own. As they grow and are schooled in the "right" way of writing, their personal voice is slowly replaced by one that sounds more like what they believe their elders expect from them. If they are allowed to develop or rediscover their own voice, their writing becomes much more personal, resulting in a more intimate author-reader relationship. Erica shows rather than tells about her sister, but her language also reveals something about herself—a distinctly personal voice:

My sister's name is Leah. She is six years old. My mom and dad think she is so sweet and kind. But the way I see it, it is a different story. You see, if I want to do something, she wants to do the same thing. And if I tell her not to touch my stuff, that is what she wants to do. She can read, but when I put a sign on my door, she ignores it and comes in anyway. So now you know my side of the story. She is a plain pest, but she is <u>my</u> sister.

Bryce's piece is more of a narrative nature, but it is also distinctly personal:

I wait silently on the side of the mat watching my friends and peers win and loss. As I am waiting for my turn thoughts and emotions race through my head. People say in many cases that the "what ifs" can make you go insane but when you wrestle you must be prepared for anything. Hearing my name over the loud speaker being announced to "the next available mat" brings a flood of emotions to my mind I think of winning and lossing of the next day at school and what I will do when I get up. I know what I will do. The second mach starts I will shoot on his leg take him down and pin him.

As I am called to the mat I act relaxed I step up and shake his hand when the referee says "wrestle" I go off on him and take him down I get over confident and he escapes. We tangle for a few seconds when suddenly he grabs me and takes me down. At his point I know that I have lost. I continue to fight but it is hopeless. The mach is over we stand up and shake hands the referee then holds up his hand. I walk of the mat defeated but my friends still respect me none the less . . .

Melinda uses the same technique in her expository piece. She selects language that is appropriate, specific, and clear, yet with a flair that is distinctly her own.

What do you think of when you hear the word, "spider?" Many people think of this little creepy, crawly thing that eats insects and sneaks up on unsuspecting people. But wait! Not all spiders are the same. Fishing spiders have the same qualities as other spiders; they have eight legs, spin their homes, and eat insects. But not all spiders live in or near water and eat fish. There are two kinds of fishing spiders, the Dolomedes and the Argyroneta. These two spiders have a lifestyle people think of for frogs or maybe snakes, but not spiders . . .

Punctuation

Punctuation may be seen as a courtesy to the reader. It tells the reader when to pause, when to assign words to dialogue rather than narration, and when two or more thoughts are specifically connected to one another. Mature authors use the conventions of punctuation as road signs in their written pieces. Without these road signs, meaning is often lost.

Nonassessable

If no punctuation is used in a piece, this aspect of writing is nonassessable. Even if they use correct sentence structure, young writers may not visually separate their thoughts. Some separate thoughts by skipping to the next line, drawing a picture, or even drawing lines between the last word of one thought and the first word of the next. If no conventional punctuation is used, the piece should be rated nonassessable. John's piece is an example:

we went on a wok to the pork we like it
I see a athr grl hes had log log har
I sad do you wot to pola he sad yes
we want to my hows we had som coco
I ast my mom if she kod slep ovr my mom sad yes I
   wos hppy

(We went on a walk to the park. We liked it. I saw another girl. She had long, long hair. I said, "Do you want to play?" She said yes. We went to my house. We had some cocoa. I asked my mom if she could sleep over. My mom said yes. I was happy.

I lat her pla weh my cat we had fon han we want to
    bad the nit woss ovr we had sow moh fon to day
The nkst mrne we wok up we had brakfist han we
    want owt it was a soniy day
its raley the end onst

I let her play with my cat. We had fun. Then we went to bed. The night was over. We had so much fun today. The next morning we woke up. we had breakfast. Then we went out. It was a sunny day. It's really the end. Honest!)

Emerging

In a piece showing an emerging sense of punctuation, the punctuation is used inconsistently to separate ideas. In this kind of piece, the author may use a period at the end of one sentence but continues the next sentence through two or more thoughts. More mature authors, in their zeal to use compound sentences, may separate sentences with commas (or nothing at all) instead of periods. Bryce's story, given on page 97, fits this description.

Developing Through Advanced

Once authors have learned to use the basic ending marks to separate ideas, they begin to learn other tools of punctuation, such as quotation marks, apostrophes, commas, and so on. While the learning of these tools doesn't necessarily have an expected sequence, they are listed here in order of their importance for communicating the sense of a piece to a reader, with the most important listed first. The appropriate use of any punctuation mark should be noted, but a piece should not be rated at the next level of development until all punctuation marks listed in the level are generally being used.

Ending marks. Writers must learn to separate ideas, whether they are simple sentences or more complex ones, by using one of three ending marks: a period, a question mark, or an exclamation point. Joseph's story about a jet should be rated at the developing level:

The Jet!

I floo in the jeat beekas it was fun.
I haf lanch in the jeat.
I see aot the windo.
I fond a new jeat.
I fly my new jeat.
I dropd a berrol.

(The Jet! I flew in the jet because it was fun. I have lunch in the jet. I see out the window. I find a new jet. I fly my new jet. I dropped a barrel.)

Apostrophes. A piece should be rated as being at the practicing level if apostrophes—along with ending marks and commas—are not only used, but used correctly, for the appropriate purposes. At first, young writers tend to use them for any word ending in *s*. Their true purpose, however, is only twofold.

Apostrophes are used to replace letters in a contraction. For this reason, teachers of young writers may call them "footprints"—they are the print left behind by the nasty thief who "stole" the letters. Adrienne shows this use of apostrophes:

> "Hello," my name is Ziggers. "what's yours?" . . .
> . . . "Why don't we just split up?"

Apostrophes are also used to show ownership (except in the word *its*). For most nouns, an apostrophe plus *s* is used to indicate the status of that noun as an owner. For plurals and other nouns ending in *s*, an apostrophe alone is used at the end of the word to show ownership. Erin's piece, reproduced in Chapter 2, uses the apostrophe to indicate possession:

> . . . Needless to say, my father's family had plenty of heated dinnertime discussions.
> . . . Meanwhile, my father was marching into Poland, following Hitler's command to invade.

Apostrophes are *not* used to indicate simple nonpossessive plurals, although many writers mistakenly use them this way. They notice an apostrophe before the end of a word ending in *s* and extend that pattern to *any* word ending in *s*.

A piece should be rated at the practicing level for use of punctuation only when apostrophes are used correctly.

Commas.   The comma is the most misunderstood, misused punctuation mark of all. Commas are used for so many different purposes (for sentences, for dates, for addresses, for lists, and so on) that writers, young and old, often place them where they don't belong and omit them where they're needed. Even experienced writers and teachers of English often disagree where they should be used.

For example, most agree that commas should be used in a series ("apples, bananas, oranges"). But many disagree whether they should be used in a series with *and* ("apples, bananas, and oranges" vs. "apples, bananas and oranges").

Most writers agree that commas should be omitted in sentences with two verbs but only one subject ("She was riding her bike and fell") and two subjects and one verb ("Riding my bike and playing hockey are my favorite pastimes"). But some may disagree over the use of commas in compound sentences ("She was riding her bike, and she fell" vs. "She was riding her bike and she fell").

Many, but not all, agree that added explanation should be set off by commas ("Added explanation, such as this phrase, should be separated from the main part of the sentence by commas"). There is also disagreement over whether to use commas to separate introductory phrases from the rest of a sentence ("Thinking she was wrong, she erased the comma").

Most agree that commas should be used along with and inside quotation marks to set off quotations, as in Dimma's piece:

> **"Oh, no. I think someone is looking at our home again," said Mother Crayon.**
>
> **"Well it will be just a minute before we will be able to go. Nobody wants to buy this old box anyway," said Father Crayon . . .**
>
> **"Well," said Sister Crayon, "I guess we don't get to go on our walk anymore. It's too late and the store is probably closed by now."**

In general, when assessing the use of the comma, both raters and authors should be in agreement about correct usage. The Modern Language Association publishes a useful manual on English usage that could be consulted, as could *The Chicago Manual of Style.*

Quotation marks.   So many young writers use dialogue that reading their pieces can be a nightmare until they learn to use quotation marks to separate the speaker's name (and other narration) from what the speaker is saying. Because of their purpose, some teachers call them "talking marks"—they go around the talking in a piece. Others call them "lips"—they are placed on either side of the words coming out of the speaker's mouth.

Adrienne uses quotation marks correctly in her story. Notice that because she does not yet use commas correctly, her piece should be rated at the developing level of punctuation. Quotation marks should be checked, however, even though they do not appear until the proficient level in the form.

> **. . . Katie yelled "I want to go home." When Katie got home, the hole was not there. Katie thought "the hole was there when I left. maybe I need to go farther ahead." So Katie hopped higher up in the mountain.**

Quotation marks, of course, are also used in expository pieces, not only to quote a person's words, but also to cite a reference from which information had been copied. Erika's expository piece, printed in Chapter 3, shows appropriate use of quotation marks:

> **"Life for me ain't been no crystal stair." In Langston Hughes poem, "Mother to Son," the mother is speaking generally to her son about the trials of life, hers in particular . . .**

Colons.   A colon is used to introduce something: a list, a long quotation, a new sentence. A colon signals that what follows it is directly related to what came just before.

Semicolons.   Semicolons are connectors; they may be used in place of a conjunction to connect two complete sentences. Abebech shows this use of a semicolon:

> **. . . It was kind of dangerous place for the crayon family to live in; their wonderful scents attracted the animals, and they wanted to eat the poor crayons.**

Semicolons also separate items in a list whose elements contain commas ("Savanna, age 10; Levi, age 8; Jacinda, age 2").

Dashes and hyphens.   A dash and a hyphen are two different things, but they are listed together here because they are often confused. The purpose of both is to separate: a dash, made up of one long horizontal line or two hyphens, is used to indicate a break in a sentence; a hyphen, made up of one short horizontal line, indicates a break in a word. A hyphen is used when a word is divided between syllables at the end of a line, and (here's a well-known fact) they are also used for some compound words—words made up of two or more separate words.

Parentheses.   Parentheses are used when an author wants to include added information (such as an explanatory phrase) that he or she does not want to treat as part of the main sentence. Parentheses help set off the information and allow for smooth reading of the sentence. Beth, in her piece on Louis Pasteur, illustrates the use of parentheses:

> **In 1854 Pasteur became professor and dean of the school of science (Faculte des scineces) at the University of Lille.**

Other marks.   Other marks of punctuation—ellipses, brackets, and single quotes—can help to add meaning or to set off information for the reader. If used, each should be used correctly before the piece can be rated at the advanced level of development for punctuation. (Again, consulting a language manual is recommended.)

*I*n order to distinguish between thoughts in a story, a mature author capitalizes the beginning of each sentence. In order to identify proper names, he or she capitalizes them. Use of capitalization, like other writing conventions, can be seen as a courtesy from author to reader.

Nonassessable

If a piece of writing contains all capital, all lowercase, or an arbitrary mix of letters, the writer's use of capitalization is nonassessable. To many young writers, a letter is a letter is a letter. They may not even realize what capital letters are or that they have a purpose. In fact, many young authors write in all capital letters, since these are the letters generally taught first at home.

More experienced writers may choose to write in all capital or all lowercase letters for effect. Whatever the reason, pieces in which capital letters are not used for their intended purpose should be rated nonassessable for capitalization.

Bianca's story about Jenny and the green ribbon, printed in Chapter 2, contains an indiscriminate mix of capital and lowercase letters, as does Kelsey's partially capitalized piece on manatees, shown in Figure 4.2. Both pieces are nonassessable as regards use of capitalization.

Emerging

A writer with an emerging sense of capitalization uses capitals inconsistently to begin sentences or distinguish names. If a writer occasionally remembers to capitalize the first word in a sentence or the proper name of a noun, and capital letters are not used inappropriately, such as in the middle of a word, capitalization should be rated as emerging. Andrew illustrates this level in his piece about himself:

I am 9. I was born on Sep 7, 1986. my mom and dad are still married. I like sports. I was born in greely. I live in greely. I like to draw. we go camping every year. I have 2 cats. I like to ride my bike. School is ok. I have 2 sisters. they are mean. we went to tucsan during spring break. my favorit food is pizza. my favorit color is green. every day we pick up Josh to take him to

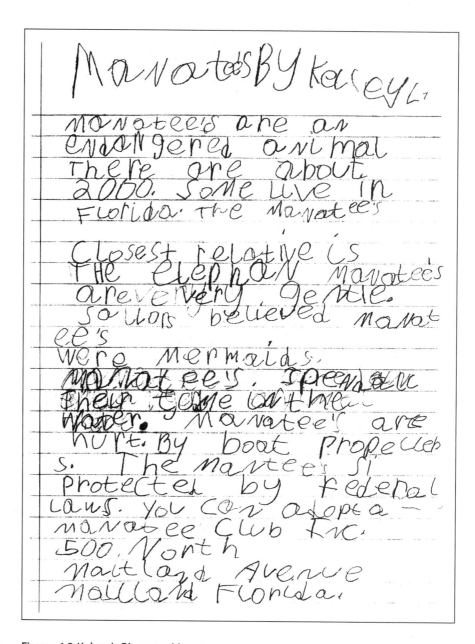

Figure 4.2 Kelsey's Piece on Manatees

school. and he takes me home. my cats names are elmo and biger. they are weird. I like to colect match box cars.

Developing Through Advanced

At more mature stages, the writer generally uses capital letters for their intended purposes. While the rater should not look for perfection, general consistency is expected. "General" consistency is somewhat subjective, but specifying a certain number of allowed errors would be difficult. Pieces vary in length, and they also vary in the number of words and purposes for which capital letters should be used. If a piece requires capitalization in a following category and only occasionally displays incorrect use of capitals for that purpose, the piece should be rated at that level.

Sentences.   All pieces require capitalization at the beginning of sentences. Any piece in which sentences are generally capitalized should be rated at the developing level.

Names.   Proper nouns in a piece should be capitalized. Proper nouns are those that establish a *specific* person (not just boy, but Tom), place (not just bank, but First National), or time (not just month, but January).

Titles.   Is the title of the piece capitalized? If it has chapters or subheadings, are they capitalized? If so, and capitalization is also correctly used for sentences and proper names, the piece should be rated as being at the practicing level. If the piece has no title or subheadings, a rating at this level cannot be determined.

Quotations.   It is difficult for young writers to remember to capitalize the first letter in a quotation, especially if the quotation begins in the middle of a sentence. Any piece containing quotations that are, in general, appropriately capitalized should be rated as proficient, *if* the preceding types of use are also capitalized correctly. If a piece has no quotations, two questions should be considered: Is it appropriate for this piece to have no quotations? Are capital letters otherwise used effectively? If the answer to both is yes, a rater may choose to write "N/A" over the box on the form that would otherwise be checked. This indicates that the student is not being rated for a tool that was not and should not have been used.

Special effects.   If a writer has mastered all the other purposes for capital letters and also uses capital letters for effect through his or her piece, he or she should be rated as advanced. A example of this is writing "BOO!" all in capital letters to emphasize surprise and/or volume.

Many young writers understand this use of capitals but have not mastered the more important ones described above. If this is the case, the rater should check this box on the Author's Profile form, but not rate the level as proficient.

Spelling

*I*f punctuation is a set of road signs on the highway of a story, then spelling allows the reader to speed along, stopping only to savor a detail or reenact an event. A mature reader uses spelling accurately so that it doesn't become an obstacle for the reader on the path toward understanding and enjoyment.

Nonassessable

If a piece is mostly undecipherable, except by the author, it should be rated as nonassessable for spelling. Ratings in other categories are based on the author's reading the piece aloud to the rater. If a piece is undecipherable even to its author, it also should be rated as being nonassessable. In order to rate Bianca's piece (also shown in Chapter 2), her teacher asked her to read it aloud:

Thea wes A be Bat Thea wes A Paba. Jena oaes wore A ran rabin. He ast Jena Wan do Yuo War That gan Rada. ol the taim. Jeny sen But thes is Not the rai tim. He gav hr Favr's Bot it Din Wort. he ask her aot to the movs Bat it diant wrk. NaoW caN You tel me way You wer that Geen ribn. No i cant it is nat the rat tim. Mene yer's past and JenY aND Jon wr gtting Old. Jeny was geting sik. The dodr Kam. They Jeny sed to Jon to unti the ribn. Wn JooN untid the ribn Jenes hed fil of.

(There was a boy, but there was a problem. Jenny always wears a green ribbon. He asked Jenny, "Why do you wear that green ribbon all the time?"

Jenny said, "But this is not the right time."

He gave her flowers, but that didn't work. He asked her out to the movies, but it didn't work. "Now you can tell me why you wear that green ribbon."

"No, I can't. It is not the right time."

Many years passed and Jenny and John were getting old. Jenny was getting sick. The doctor came. Then Jenny said to John to untie the ribbon. When John untied the ribbon Jenny's head fell off.)

Emerging

If personal, or nonconventional, spelling is used within a piece, but some letter-sound association is evident, spelling can be rated as at the emerging level. At this level, the reader should be able to decipher what is being said, though it takes effort to do so. Kelsey, for example, uses personal spelling in her piece, but it is decipherable:

Wen my dad dihd we wet to the funarol. Then we wet home. I rot a llat to the mamoral. My dad dide bkasa of agn orng.

(When my dad died we went to the funeral. Then we went home. I wrote a letter to the Memorial. My dad died because of Agent Orange.)

Developing

When a piece contains enough conventional spelling for it to be easily read, the spelling is at the developing level. Whitney's piece on scientists and their work is at this level:

> Scientist use bottals of stuf to make formulas and stuf for other things. They discover lots and lots of stuf and sometimes make inventions of stuf.

Practicing

If the spelling in a piece is generally conventional, it can be rated at the practicing level. At this level, most of the words are spelled correctly. An occasional error pops up, but only upon careful reading. Matt's piece on television illustrates this level:

> I think T.V. is a great influence of our lives today. Not only does it give us entertainment value, it also gives us many other values like education and religion.
>
> Still another value is the travel aspect. Alot of elder people cannot go to certian places of the world they would like to go to. With just one, easy flip of the switch, you are there. Some of the most beautiful places in the world are televised on the Discovery Cannel and it will tell you more than you could ever know about the place you would like to visit. It will also show you sights you could never see if you went in person anyway.
>
> Let's move on to the religous aspect of T.V. On some channels, religous programs are televised regularly. Some people can't go to mass or service, but with one easy flip of the switch, you can be at the mass. The mass is not only easy to do, it is also held at the most beautiful churches in the world.
>
> Continuing on to the educational content, we see many programs that help little children learn things they need to know before going into preschool. My aunt is now taking a class that is on television. That's right! It is a half an hour class every morning that she tapes and watches later. All she has to do is write down her assignments down, and occasionally come in for a pop-quiz.
>
> Entertainment is the best though. It can broadcast many shows to keep children of all ages entertained. The T.V. can also give family value by giving good programs that the family can sit down and watch together. Sometimes a movie will be shown, right in the luxury of your own home.
>
> Now I know that some people think that telvision encourages violence but I respectfully disagree. There was alot of violence before TV, so I don't

see what is so bad. But if you don't wan't your child watching that junk, have them change the channel or get a ban from that channel.

All in all, I think television is great. It helps little children mentally grow and let people see the world without ever leaving their home. It lets people go to mass and gives great entertainment values. I you do not want your child watching certain channels, just simply get a parental ban. I think television is great in many ways, aspects, and values. I really enjoy T.V., and I hope you do too.

Proficient

Spelling is rated as proficient when the piece contains consistently conventional spelling. At this point, the piece is basically flawless regarding spelling. Whether the author is simply a good speller or has used a dictionary, spell checker, or other resource, spelling errors have been corrected. If they are careful editors, even very young students can be rated at this level. Connor's piece is brief but flawless:

Hello, I'm running for President of the class. I will try to be the best I can be, and that's a goal I can fulfill! And I will help people with their jobs and help people if they have a problem. And I would help you if you needed it. I will be a good representative in student council. I will listen to you.

Advanced

At the advanced level, the spelling in the piece is consistently conventional, even for technical vocabulary. There is a fine line between proficient and advanced levels of spelling. At the highest level, teachers expect consistently correct spelling for edited pieces. Advanced writers edit their work consistently and also strive for sophisticated vocabulary, even if the words are more difficult to spell. In expository papers for such content areas as science or math, writers who choose not to shy away from technical vocabulary stretch their spelling skills. Pieces that contain this kind of vocabulary and are consistently correct should be considered at the advanced level. High-level vocabulary can also be used in narrative pieces, as shown in Nicole's piece, which follows. Use of such words as *triumph*, *meandered*, *prototype*, and *boulevard* shows that Nicole does not limit her vocabulary for ease in spelling:

Beep! My alarm radio sounded. I awoke with a start. As I gazed around sleepily, I could see sunlight streaming into my room. In a triumph of effort, I hoisted myself out of bed and sighed.

After dressing, I meandered down the stairs into the kitchen. My teacher, Beverly, was sitting and enjoying her morning cup of coffee.

"Good morning sleepy-head," she warmly greeted me.

"Hello Bev," I replied.

We chatted over cereal about the tasks that lay ahead: writing a press release for Apple, observing a board meeting, installing software, and working on the prototype for the latest Apple computer.

As anyone can see, I was definitely not a student in a normal school. Because of my grades, I was in a special tutoring program for good students. Living away from home for a year, I learned about a career that I planned to follow. The program was fashioned after the apprentice days of Europe. Even though I missed my family, I enjoyed my work with Bev. She treated me like one of her own.

After breakfast, I piled all of my equipment into Beverly's station wagon and we drove to the Apple building. As we cruised down the boulevard, I gazed at the lush vegetation on either side.

We parked the car and walked inside. Upon entering, I presented my identification badge to the security guard, and we walked down the hall to Beverly's office, room 7306. Apple was currently working on the prototype for a new machine, Rhapsody. Scheduled to be out in late 1998, it would put all other machines to shame. My first task, at hand, was to type a press-release about Rhapsody for various magazines. As I sat down at my Power Mac, I thanked myself for taking AP English the previous year. After tediously working for an hour, I presented my work to Bev. She immediately approved and faxed my work to Apple CEO, Gilbert Amillio. Within weeks, my press release would be published in several Mac magazines.

Lunch was fulfilling as usual. The food was, as always, much better than my school's cafe. I could not complain. When I finished eating, I hurried to the fifth floor. I was late to a meeting. Sitting down hurriedly, I greeted Beverly. Just then, Gilbert Amillio called the meeting to order. The topic was Rhapsody. As people offered suggestions about the next course for Apple to take, I furiously scribbled on my memo pad. The date for Rhapsody's debut was finally scheduled.

By the time the meeting adjourned, it was very late. Driving home with Beverly, I suddenly realized how tired I had become. I thought about my apprenticeship. My year at Apple was almost through. I would miss all of my co-workers, but I kept up hope. Because of my apprenticeship, I would be guaranteed a job at Apple in the future.

I ate a hurried dinner. After it was finished, I said good night to Bev and plodded upstairs. I tiredly put my pajamas on and curled up with the latest issue of MacWorld magazine.

The conventions of writing must be learned and followed if a writer is to be respected for his or her thoughts. However, this chapter was included *after* more content-based authoring skills for a specific reason: *the conventions are not the first or most important aspect of writing that should be evaluated.* Authors generally write and revise with communication of ideas foremost in their minds. Effective communication is the priority; editing for conventions should add polish to an already well-designed piece.

W hat does the Author's Profile look like when in use? This chapter analyzes the writing of two children, Curt and Haley. Their writing was assessed over a two-year period. One narrative and one expository rubric was used for each child, containing assessments of pieces written over the entire period. Each evaluated piece is transcribed here exactly as it was written.

Curt and Haley both entered our team-taught second-third-fourth-grade classroom as second graders in the same year. Although they were the same age and in the same grade, these young writers began at very different developmental stages of writing.

Upon entering the class, Haley was a verbal, outgoing young girl who loved conversation and drama. Curt was shy and quiet. He wanted so badly to be successful he refused to ask for help, thinking it would make him look bad. Haley's goal at the beginning of the year was to write many stories. She would crank them out as quickly as possible, adding them to her "Pieces I've Written" list. She ignored the Author's Checklists in favor of finishing more pieces. Curt's goal, on the other hand, was perfection. He used the Author's Checklists from the very beginning. He wasn't about to leave anything out of his stories. His "sloppy copies" contained cross-outs, changes, and added details. He worked on his first story until after Christmas, when I finally told him he had to quit, finished or not, and begin editing so he could publish it.

Once Haley made the transition from personal narrative to creative story writing, she was both in and out of her element. She loved to use her imagination, so coming up with original ideas was never a problem. She was fascinated by Laura Ingalls Wilder, and her stories were always set in pioneer America. Haley wanted to develop each of her ideas as fully as those in the novels she loved to read. Unfortunately, when her use of conventions and her ability to get things down on paper didn't match her ability to develop a knockout story, she found herself forced to use fewer words and leave out some needed events. As a result, her later narrative stories, such as "The Houses that Live," were often built around long, rambling stretches of dialogue.

Curt, on the other hand, wrote what he knew. His stories would always involve a safe, well-known subject with a twist. When I discovered he was beginning a second story about football—he had just spent months working on his first story about the same topic—I worried that he was in a rut. He worked hard to make the second story different from his first, building especially on the beginning and the problem. When I asked him to try a subject other than realistic fiction, he worked for months on "Killer Men," a sequel to a story written by one of his friends.

Both Curt and Haley seemed to create expository writing more easily. They enjoyed organizing their longer writing into chapters, giving them the needed structure for developing them. Haley worked harder in her expository pieces to edit her writing, asking for peer (and adult) help several times along the way. For both, their research-based expository writing tended to be more fully developed than their persuasive pieces, while their persuasive pieces had stronger thesis statements.

Curt's and Haley's writing was assessed over a three-year period on the same rubric. You will find narrative and expository rubrics for each child on the following pages. Only two of the pieces were assigned: they were required to write a report on a planet (they both happened to choose Jupiter). There were also required to write an "If I Were President" piece, persuading either the class or the country to vote for them. The other expository pieces were written as part of each student's Personal Learning Plan (a goal set to learn about a particular topic). The topics of the narrative pieces were all free choice. Each evaluated piece is included exactly the way it was written. Curt and Haley began at different places in writing, though they were the same age. You will discover that Haley, in both narrative and expository writing, is beginning to close the gap between them.

The pages that follow contain all of Curt's assessed pieces, then all of Haley's. The completed Author's Profiles for each child can be found at the end of the chapter. The numbers in circles on those completed forms refer to the number of each piece. There are several ways you could use these pieces of writing. Why not copy the rubrics in the Appendix and try rating these pieces yourself? How do your ratings compare to the ones at the end of the chapter? See if you can determine what you might work on next with Curt and Haley. How would the information from these rubrics translate into letter grades for writing (if you are required to submit letter grades)? Think about how a student-led conference could work if a student had the rubric in hand to discuss his or her writing or how mini-lessons or individual conferences might be planned for writing class. Think about how students could set goals for their writing development based on what is indicated on the rubric. And think about how you could illustrate growth, even in a student who is really struggling or a student who may think no growth is needed. We have not even begun to use the rubrics to their full potential, but we are beginning to discover the power they hold for teachers and students.

Curt

Narrative Piece 1

I Wint to College

I wint to Notre Dame to ask if I could play football. I sdad in a doorme. I hade to study a lot. Win it was football soesin I wand to play football. the caoch side yes I was namebr 25 I was wid resevr and ranning bake. I hade to paraktis a lot. I was the best playr on the teme. are frst game was on Apral 17 1994 are game was at home and at 2:00 pm we war in the lakr room waiting for the game. we went out of the tunnel we war playing agist msagin. We kikt off to the 10 yard lin. Frst tha past tha got to the 16 yard lin. Then the quardrback got sakt he lost 1 or 2 yards. Seth hit the quardrbak on the 3rd down. tha had to punt the ball. I got the ball. I broka through the line. I ran down the sid lin. I got bake to the 50 yard lin. then we lind up. The qodr bake throw the ball to me I cat the ball. Seth blakt for me. the refaree thaow flags I got takld the refary cuald a penalte it was a 10 yard penalte. We lind up agin me and seth wer on the left sid we went up the side and the qodrbak thror the ball to me.

(I went to Notre Dame to ask if I could play football. I stayed in a dorm. I had to study a lot. When it was football season I wanted to play football. The coach said yes! I was number 25. I was wide receiver and running back. I had to practice a lot. I was the best player on the team. Our first game was on April 17, 1994. Our game was at home and at 2:00 P.M. We were in the locker room waiting for the game. We went out of the tunnel. We were playing against Michigan. We kicked off to the 10-yard line. First they passed. They got to the 16-yard line. Then the quarterback got sacked. He lost 1 or 2 yards. Seth hit the quarterback on the third down. They had to punt the ball. I got the ball. I broke through the line. I ran down the side line. I got back to the 50-yard line. Then we lined up. The quarterback threw the ball to me. I caught the ball. Seth blocked for me. The referee threw flags. I got tackled. The referee called a penalty. It was a 10-yard penalty. We lined up again. Seth and I were on the left side. We went up the side and the quarterback threw the ball to me.)

I cat the ball. I got to the 35 yard lin then I got tacald then I lind up as a running bak. Seth lind up as a wid resevr. the qodrbak was bak, seth went out he cat the ball. We went out again. me and seth ran rit by eachather. The dfinsiv bak omost hit us and we hit ech other. Seth cat the ball. Then he fmbald. I recavrd the ball. I got a frst down. At the 25 yard lin. Then we went with out a hadal. We ran out. The quarterback through the ball. And the defense intercepted the ball. And they ran it back for a touchdown 14 minute later. The score was 13 to 12 ther faver. We wer at the 25 yard lin. ther were 5 seconds left. I new we had to go for the hail mary. we lind up with 4 wid resevrs on one side. I was one of them and Seth was one of them too the quarterback through the ball to the end zone and I cat it in the end zone. And we won. I cat the final touchdown. I falt very good. Bekus we wer playing the orange boull. And the final score was 19 to 13. The End.

I caught the ball. I got to the 35-yard line. Then I got tackled. Then I lined up as a running back. Seth lined up as a wide receiver. The quarterback went back. Seth went out. He caught the ball. We went out again. Seth and I ran right by each other. The defensive back almost hit us, and we hit each other. Seth caught the ball. Then he fumbled. I recovered the ball. I got a first down at the 25-yard line. Then we went without a huddle. We ran out. The quarterback threw the ball, and the defense intercepted the ball. And they ran it back for a touchdown 14 minutes later. The score was 13 to 12 their favor. We were at the 25-yard line. There were 5 seconds left. I knew we had to go for the Hail Mary. We lined up with four wide receivers on one side. I was one of them and Seth was one of them too. The quarterback threw the ball to the end zone, and I caught it in the end zone. And we won. I caught the final touchdown. I felt very good because we were playing the Orange Bowl. And the final score was 19 to 13. The End.)

Narrative Piece 2

My Senior Year

Today was the football game. It was time for us to run out of the tunnel. It was my senior year in college. We ran out of the tunnel like a herd of buffalo.

The referee flipped the coin. I called heads. Guess what it was . . . tails.

They kicked off. Seth and I were back to return the kick off. I caught the ball. I thought about what it would be like to beat Nebraska.

I almost got tackled, and I got tripped up. I got hit very hard.

We got into a new formation with wide receivers on the right side. Seth and I were two of them. I thought about my broken knee.

The wide receivers criss-crossed. The quarterback almost got sacked, so he ran. He got two or three yards.

We lined up in the same line up. We criss-crossed. This time the quarterback threw the ball to me or Seth—we didn't know. So I reached out for it and then . . .

. . . I got hit so hard I flipped over on my head. The next thing I knew I was in the hospital.

I watched the game. The score was 21 to 20, their favor. There was about

20 seconds left in the fourth quarter. We had the ball. We had to do a field goal. We took our last time out. We brought on the field goal.

The kick was up. They got a fingertip unit. I was so mad at myself for losing the game. We lost the game!

Then I went to sleep.

Narrative Piece 3

Killer Men

Hi it's us again, we are hiding in our cabin. It's cool in the cabin. We have 4 TV's in the cabin. We also have six ATV's. All of them are green. Josh is tall and has brown eyes that look like hot cocoa. Josh as blond hair that's back in a pony tail. Michael has brown eyes and he has black hair.

Josh said, "I'm going to the store, and if I'm not back in one hour wait. What do I need to get?"

"Pizza and games and pop," I answered. "Josh."

"What"

"Stop, come back in."

"Why?"

"Because I see two faces."

"OK, OK."

"Let's go downstairs to the sacirady control system." We heard the sound of glass breaking, so we ran all the way to the stairs. We ran down the wooden stars like we were racing. We turned left into the room and turned on the lights. It looked like two red eyes were looking at us. They were not here before.

Some strange voice said, "Push the button. Push it." Then Josh said, "Guys, it's just me"

"Oh good it's you. OK, one of us is going to go up there," I whispered.

"Not me," a small voice answered.

"Not me," said Michael.

"But it's so, so creepy up there. O-o-o-k." So I crept up the stairs and looked, but I did not see a thing. They took all the food.

"OK, I'm going in the black Lamborgini," said Josh, and he hopped in the car.

"Man," I said. "Three hours went by like days. We need Josh. I wonder where Josh is? I'll go to the store. I'll get Josh."

I took the Porsche. When I got into town I saw the two men in the Lamborgini, so I went to the store and asked somebody who worked there, "Did you see a kid who has a Seattle Supersonics hat on?"

"Yes, I have. Was he with two men?"

"Yes."

I ran and got into the Porsche. The sun was beating down on me and the seats were as sticky as honey. I saw Josh fall out of the door. He got up and opened the door of the Porsche.

"Move over! Let me drive. You don't have your driver's license."

"No. But we found you, didn't we?"

"Yes. Let's go back and get some food."

And so we did. Who knows? They could come after you.

Narrative Piece 4

Christmas

It was Christmas eve and my friends were over. I was going to sleep when I heard something on the roof. I got up and stepped over my friends in their sleeping bags. They were so close together I tripped over Josh, he woke up. Then everybody woke up because of the sound. Then I told them about the sound I heard.

"Let's go," I said

So we went down stairs and hid behind the Christmas tree. All ten eyes were on the fire place. Then we saw two black boots, then a body. He was a little man dressed in white and red. He was Santa Claus! "I have to get his autograph" Josh said.

"NO, you can't"

"But this is going to be my first time and my last time to see him" and so he started to walk and we grabbed onto his boxers but he dragged us behind him.

Santa Claus looked over at us "see, now look what you got us into," I said. Santa Claus smiled at that.

We all ran off, but Josh stayed to get Santa Claus's autograph. Then I woke up and all of my friends woke up too. I said, "I had this really cool dream that we saw Santa Claus."

"I had the same dream," Connor said.

"Me to," said Clay.

"I did to," said Seth.

"Josh, what does that piece of paper say?" I asked.

"It is Santa Claus's autograph," he answered.

Narrative Piece 5

Mountain Climbing

"Riley hang on we will get you for the 35th time!" Clay grumbled.

"We should never have brought you mountain climbing, you always get stuck," Curt yelled. "Help me, Help me," Riley said. so Clay and Curt helped

Riley up and by the time Riley got up he all ready had started to look at the rock for the science project he was doing for school.

"It really gets late faster then in the supper," Savanna said.

"What time is it," Clay said. They got camp set up in a matter of minutes. They started a fire so they could stay warm from the heavy over cast. They were eating when they heard a sound off to the right. "It sounds like a storm," Riley said. So they got into their tents. In the tent that Riley was in with Curt and Clay Riley kept on talking about what he thought what kind of a storm it was going to be. After a while he went to sleep but Curt and Clay were still awake talking. They decided to go out in the blazing storm to see if everything was ok. When they got outside it was raining so hard they could barely see two feet in front of them. Curt was the stronger of the two, so when they got outside and had to move the heavy stuff Curt did it.

We forgot a back pack out in the storm. "It's over hear," Clay pointed to a back pack. "It is a Coleman green and black back pack" Clay yelled at the top of his lungs just to be able to talk to Curt. All the sudden a tree fell. Clay tried to get out of the way but it fell on him. It wast a big tree but big enough to keep him so he couldn't get it off by himself. I ran over to Clay and started to get the tree of Clay. After Curt got the tree off Clay they both ran to the tent. Once inside the tent they both crawled into there sleeping bags and fell fast to sleep. In the morning Riley got out of bed and got dressed and came out of his tent. Everybody else was up and eating breakfast.

"Hi Riley do you know were the compass is?" Mary said

"Ah ah ah No."

"You mean we do not have the compass" Clay said in shock.

"It was in a back pack that was green and black and was a Coleman back pack." said Riley.

It fell off the cliff last night Clay said. Me and Clay traded glances.

"We can tell by which way the sun comes up" Clay added.

"Ok pack up and don't panic" Curt said. So they packed up. After they packed up they all decided which way to go and started. After we walked about two or three miles we were walking by a cliff and Riley was closest to the edge. Then Riley slipped and started to fall. Me and Clay dove for him I was the bigger of the two so I knocked him out of the way and got Riley. He was barley hanging on. All the sudden the wind picked up it was like all the sudden somebody turned on a big fan. I pulled Riley up and we all looked and a rescue helicopter.

"We'r saved Savanna said with joy. As it landed we ran to it. When we got on the pilot took off.

"Guys, let's go up way back in to the Alaska mountains" Savanna said.

"OK" Mary said.

Expository Piece 1

Jupiter

This report is about the planet Jupiter. Jupiter is a giant planet. Larger and heavier than all the other planets combined.

You can see Jupiter's sixteen moons through a small telescoope. Stell Jupiter has at least 16 moons. One of Jupiter's moons is called the Pizza moon. Also with Jupiter's 16 moons there is a reing.

If Jupiter were hollo, more then 1,400 planet Earths could fit inside. No one has seen what Jupiter is like beneath it's clouds. Jupiter's year is 4380 days. Next to Jupiter the other planets shrink.

The red spot seems to be a long lasting storm. The scientists have watched the red spot for more then 200 years the scientists think the red spot is a storm and gases.

I hoped you liked my report. it would be fun to fly passed Jupiter and see it's many moons, rings and spot. It would take many Earth years but even less Jupiter years to get there.

Expository Piece 2

How to Identify Poudre Canyon Evergreens

Evergreens in this group may have either very very short pine needles or scales that look like those on a snake. Instead of pine cones, they ay have small berries that look like blueberries. This is either a Juniper or a Red Cedar.

This evergreen is a shurb with needs a that are 5–14mm long. It may have berries. This shrub only grows 2–3 feet tall. This is a common Juniper.

This evergreen is a small tree that has scales like a snake. It may have berries too. This is a red cedar.

The pine needles on the grown-up trees in this group look like regular needles and they have pine cones instead of berries. The pine needles have sheaths at the bottom and they are usually in the groups of two or more. The pine cones have scales that are very thick and woody. These trees are in the pine group.

The pine needles are not sheathed at the bottom and they are not in groups. The pine cone sclaes are not very thick or woody. The older branches have "stumps" from fallen needles that look like goosebumps. This is either an Engelmann or a Blue Spruce.

The ends of the pine needles are not very sharp to touch. The pine cones are about 5 cm long and they have scales that are rounded at the tip. This is an Engelmann Spruce.

If the pine needles are stiff and spine-tipped to touch. The pine cones are about 8 cm long and they have scales that are more flattened at the tip. This is a Blue Sprice. The Blue Spruce is Colorado's state tree.

The older branches are smooth. The pine cones hang downward and they have thin, flattened, pointed pieces that stick out like rattails. This is a Douglas Fir.

The pine needles are very very long and are in two's or three's. The pine needles are crowded at the end of the branches and are covered by a sheath. This is a Ponderosa Pine.

The trees are tall and slender with pine needles in pairs and scattered along the branches. The pine cones stay on the tree for several years. This is a lodgepole pine. These trees were used by the Indians to make teepees.

Expository Piece 3

The Battle of Vicksburg

It started in 1861 whan 11 southern states left the U.S. They left because Abraham Lincoln was elected President and he wanted to get rid of slavery. The South wanted slavery but the North did not want slavery so they went to war over it. Both teams thought it was going to be a short war but it lasted 4 years.

Chapter One: What led up to the Battle of Vicksburg

The town of Vicksburg, Mississippi was a very important city in the civil war.

In April, Admiral Farragut captured New Orleans at the mouth of the mississippi.

The South could not get their supplies up and down the river.

The union wanted to take over Vicksburg because they could not control the South without having control of the Mississippi River and the railroads along the river.

Vicksburg was founded in 1814 by Newet Vick. It was high on a bluss and on the east side of the Mississippi River.

After a small fight at Vicksburg between the two sides, Farragut had to withdraw his ships and return to New Orleans.

Chapter Two: In the Battle of Vicksburg

In the battle, some of the citizens lived in caves dug into the bluffs. These caves provided protection in the battle. You can still see these caves today.

On the river, by Vicksburg, there was a hair pin turn so the North had to slow down. That made ships an easy target.

Instead of going straight to Vicksburg, Grant, the general of the North, headed for Jackson, the State Capital 35 miles down the river.

When Grant landed, he only had three days of rations and ammunition. In less then 3 weeks Grant won 5 battles.

When the spring rains flooded the Yazoo River, it exposed Vicksburg to an emphibious attack but when they tried they got stuck so they tried to back out but the South had started to chop down trees so the had to walkout.

Grant beat the confederates at Point Gipsin on May 1. Grant went on to beat them at Raymond and at Jackson.

Grant did not intend to hold on to Jackson. With Jeffersons army out of the way, he turned and started for Vicksburg.

In the battle of Vicksburg, Grant was so close to the Confederates. Just a short walk and a pair of glasses would bring Vicksburgs River banks into focus.

Fred Grant, U.S. Grant's son, was wounded at Big Black River. All thought all of the kids went home with Julia, Grant's wife.

Chapter Three: Affects of the Battle

After the war ended, the communities had to rebuils levies and had to replant things and reharvest crops.

After the war, houses were burned down and houses were blown apart. After the war a lot of people lost their stuff.

The steamboat industry came back very rapidly and was very important to the rebirth of Vicksburg.

Thirteen years after the war, the river reshaped and Vicksburg had to have the Engineers fix it so Vicksburg could still be a docking area.

The Mississippi River did what the North could not do. The River cut across DeSoto Peninsula, braking DeSoto Point and destroying what was left of Vicksburg, Shreiveport and Texas railroad.

Conclusion:

The Battle of Vicksburg was one of many battles that played a major role in the cival war. It was a war over a town on the Mississippi River.

Expository Piece 4

If I Were President

If I were president I would temporarily raise taxes. We need to balance the budget and not spend more money than we have.

I think we need to balance the budget by cutting some government stuff, like not paying people who don't work unless they are old or disabled. I think we need to cut back on military unless we are at war.

I think we need to spend more money in education so that more adults will get jobs. Another benefit is people are smarter and make more inventions. This makes life easier.

I think we should also spend more money on crime so there are fewer robberies and killings. This can be done by controlling gangs.

Expository Piece 5

Shunda's Newsstand

I will tell you what I learned about making good business desisions from reading Shundas news stand. A gain is when you end up haveing more then you started with. A loss is when you do not have as much money as you started with. A profit is the money that you have after you've payed back loans if you have any. I learned how to use a graph of how many newspapers she sold and how many she didn't sell. I learned how to find out how many prodks to buy/make. Sometimes the more prodaks you buy/make the more you have left over. I learned how to make and read a table that tells how many newspaper she sold and how many she didn't sell. These are all the many things I learned from reading Shunda's news stand.

Haley

Narrative Piece 1

Maggie and Haley Played Together

We colr at napt uktim.
than we eat sak.
than it was cenup tim.
than we went to lash.

(We colored at independent work time.
Then we ate snack.
Then it was clean-up time.
Then we went to lunch.)

Narrative Piece 2

Haley First Walked

When I frst wokt, my pairns camdlt I wokt away. My brother castst me. I scam! I wntd to wok mor! We went home. I went to bad niut niut.

(When I first walked, my parents clapped. I walked away. My brother caught me. I screamed! I wanted to walk more! I went to bed. Night-night.)

Narrative Piece 3

I Met Breann

(The underlined words in this story indicate words that Haley had circled in her draft as words she knew needed "grown-up" help.)

I met Breann on a sunny day. I got an ice cream cone. She had a Happy mell. I hav the <u>rast</u> of <u>man</u> to my mom. We went down the <u>slad</u>. Breann <u>hrt</u> her <u>ame</u> so we <u>cad</u> not play. I sat and <u>fnshed</u> my ice crem cone. a week latr I met her <u>agen</u> at school. We <u>fned</u> out she was in my <u>clas</u>. We have <u>ban</u> frands <u>snis</u>.

(I met Breann on a sunny day. I got an ice cream cone. She had a Happy Meal. I gave the rest of mine to my mom. We went down the slide. Breann hurt her arm, so we could not play. I sat and finished my ice cream cone. A week later I met her again at school. We found out she was in my class. We have been friends since.)

Narrative Piece 4

The Houses that Live

One ordinary day a girl about 16 was out walking. After her walk she desisted to see her friend. So she went to the little straw house and said hello is Leah, there was no answer. Iliana waited she asked again is Leah there no repeal then something was on her back. She new rite away it was her little sitter Sarah. Sitter get off me and tell me why you left Kaleb. And how did you find me. you're blue eyes, and you're bade hear. Wheres Kaleb? Well I went out to get some river water and wan I came back the door was looked. Her baby brother was left alone! Ilianas hart began to pound. "Did you not cheek it" "I did" "Wait about the key did you tray to an look it" "yes but it would not an look. "Do you know if you left the window open? asked Iliana. Yes . . . well let's go." Iliana inerupted. I'll rase! OK! Wan they got there kaleb was crying the went to the window "fewhh", its open.

(One ordinary day a girl about sixteen was out walking. After her walk she decided to see her friend. So she went to the little straw house and said, "Hello, is Leah there?" There was no answer. Iliana waited. She asked again, "Is Leah there?" There was no reply.

Then something was on her back. She knew right away it was her little sister Sarah. "Sister, get off me and tell me why you left Kaleb. And how did you find me?"

"Your blue eyes and your blond hair," [replied Sarah].

"Where's Kaleb?" [asked Iliana.] "Well, I went out to get some river water and when I came back the door was locked," [answered Sarah]. Her baby brother was left alone! Iliana's heart began to pound.

"Did you not check it?"

"I did!"

"What about the key, did you try to unlock it?"

"Yes, but it would not unlock."

"Do you know if you left the window open?" asked Iliana.

"Yes . . ."

"Well, let's go," Iliana interrupted.

"I'll race you!" [said Sarah.]

"Okay!" [Iliana agreed.] When they got there Kaleb was crying. They went to the window. "Phew, it's open.")

They jumped in and calmed Kaleb than that was that the girls asked themselvs. You mast feed me you mast feed me. It mast be in my mind remarked Iliana. Sister Sister we need to repair are house. I'll go get shingles and I'll start harvesting ok. Opps Kaleb. Taking Kaleb with her. She had almost forgot him. In about 4 weeks the harvest was done. Than it was time to make preserves no one had time to play in a couple weeks it was time to sew. When that was finished time to get the rest of the sun. They got some water to splash on each other. Then they jumped rope I'll get a vine decided Sarah. Ok, they played for awhile than something hoped out from the bak of them. epee. Wt am co. Leah! Iliana sad happily. "I'm back" said Leah. I had to see Ben, and I helped him with harves. we need to do mine now my sister well help. I'll repair you're house. The next day they started when Ilian got on the roof in a instant she was on the ground. finely she finished. She would do the sowing that night it then they walked home. thy herd repenting. Cold Cold how awaful Sarah said I'm going to see how the town is doing ok be back sown. And she was. in a instant she was there. Sarah you're back so sown the haves are a live yelled Sarah. no there not come in bed before you frees replied Iliana. ok well so some tomorrow ok "I'm making a patch work quilt for ma and pa." I'll finish my patch work quilt for us. said Sarah. ok, I'll hurry to get ma's and pa's dome so I can help you. ok, but what about Kaleb's I'll do his now ok. ok. so they stated the patch work Ilana was on the 156 patch I'll start denier now.

They jumped in and calmed Kaleb. Then "What was that?" the girls asked themselves.

"You must feed me, you must feed me."

"It must be in my mind," remarked Iliana.

"Sister, sister we need to repair our house. I'll go get shingles," [said Sarah].

"And I'll start the harvesting, okay?" [said Iliana.] "Oops, Kaleb." Iliana took Kaleb with her. She had almost forgotten him.

In about 4 weeks the harvest was done. Then it was time to make preserves. No one had time to play. In a couple of weeks it was time to sew. When that was finished it was time to enjoy the rest of the sun. They got some water to splash on each other. Then they jumped rope. "I'll get a vine," decided Sarah.

"Okay."

They played for a while, then something hopped out from the back of them. "Epee. Wit am co," [Leah shouted (in another language)].

"Leah!" Iliana said happily.

"I'm back," said Leah. "I had to see Ben, and I helped him with harvest. We need to do mine now."

"My sister will help. I'll repair your house," [said Iliana].

The next day they started. When Iliana got on the roof in an instant she was on the ground. Finally she finished. She would do the sewing that night. Then they walked home.

They heard [the house] repeating, "Cold. Cold. How awful."

Sarah said, "I'm going to see how the town is doing."

"Okay. Be back soon," [agreed Iliana]. And she was. In an instant she was there. "Sarah! You're back so soon," [said Iliana].

"The houses are alive!" yelled Sarah.

"No, they're not. Come into bed before you freeze!" replied Iliana.

"Okay," [said Sarah].

"We'll sew some tomorrow," said Iliana.

"Okay."

"I'm making a patchwork quilt for Ma and Pa."

"I'll finish my patchwork quilt for us," said Sarah.

"Okay. I'll hurry to get Ma's and Pa's done so I can help you."

"Okay, but what about Kaleb's?"

"I'll do his now, okay?"

"Okay."

So they started the patchwork. Iliana was on the 156th patch. "I'll start dinner now," [said Iliana].

I'll get working. said Sarah. for denier they would have slat park sow after diner they have supper so went supper came they wear warty when they heard a sound. you're going to bran me. Stop stop. You're going to barn me. stop. stop. Sarah you go out and see waits happen ok. ok. so she went out to have a look. Than she ran into the house and happed in bad. Tell me why you raced in like a elephant. Th-th-the how-how-house is a live! no it's not you probate saw same thing. Now let's eat super. ok. after super time to go to bad they took off there dresses and put on the night gowns and happed in bed. Then whet was that thay asked themselvs she was right I'm a live the house said. Sarah i guess that you Right. Iliana was scared. you have any ideas Iliana. Ya I'm going to cut the face out.

"I'll get working," said Sarah.

For dinner they would have salt pork. So after dinner they have supper. So when supper came they were ready when they heard a sound.

"You're going to burn me! Stop! Stop! You're going to burn me! Stop! Stop!" [a voice yelled.]

"Sarah, you go out and see what's happening, Okay?"

"Okay." So she went out to have a look. Then she ran into the house and hopped in bed.

"Tell me why you raced in like an elephant."

"Th-th-the how-how-house is alive!"

"No, it's not. You probably saw something. Now let's eat supper."

"Okay."

After supper it was time to go to bed. They took off their dresses and put on their nightgowns and hopped into bed.

Then "What was that?" they asked themselves.

"She was right! I'm alive," the house said.

"Sarah, I guess that you were right." Iliana was scared.

"Do you have any ideas, Iliana?"

"Yeah. I'm going to cut the face out," Iliana said.

Narrative Piece 5

Grumpy learns His Lesson

Grumpy was about 9. He had a sister about 13 her name is Maryin they call her Mary for short. she was beautiful she had brown here and green eyes and Grumpy had a sister her name is grace she is 5 the youngest she had gold her and blue eyes Mary liked being the oldest but Grumpy was mean he took mary and grace's money and toys when Christmas came, and he pushed and shoved to be the first one and when the girls were in bed he took a rope and tide their hear and pulled the rope and he did not tell it was him he told that the neighbor had done it mary had to tell Grace that Grumpy was doing it but when She told Grace Grumpy was right there and told Grace that the neighbor was responsible for the things and he didn't do it and Grace believed Grumpy was furious at Mary and told their Ma and Pa that Mary had ripped their school books on purpose and blamed him for it. then when ma and pa decided that they

(Grumpy was about nine. He had a sister who was about thirteen. Her name was Marian. They called her Mary for short. She was beautiful. She had brown hair and green eyes, and Grumpy had a sister whose name was Grace. She was five, the youngest. She had gold hair and blue eyes.

Mary liked being the oldest, but Grumpy was mean. He took Mary's and Grace's money and toys when Christmas came, and he pushed and shoved to be the first one. When the girls were in bed he took a rope and tied their hair and pulled the rope. He did not tell it was him. He told that the neighbor had done it. Mary had to tell Grace that Grumpy was doing it, but when she told Grace Grumpy was right there and told Grace that the neighbor was responsible for the things and he didn't do it.

Grace believed Grumpy, who was furious at Mary and told their Ma and Pa that Mary had ripped their school books on purpose and blamed him for it. Then when Ma and Pa decided would have to punish her "She said that Grumpy told a lie" and she showed the books in the dresser," and they were not there "she said, they she put them there when she came home from school she put them books right her" Than she looked in Grumpy room and there they were under Grumpy bed Ma and Pa were amassed that grumpy had done the lie they were mad to they had to punish him but how, Mary new they would act like they never know! but Grace, she believed Grumpy. How would they convents her! So they had to do something else. But what! In a few days Laura & Carie Mary's friends thought they should play a joke a him. They thought that it was wonderful But how would they do it? Mary thought they should take his favorite thing, but that was not good enough. So they thought again then they had it Mary would pretend to be sick and when Grumpy came in shoe would jump up right when he was doing the trick and she would "say I'm the ghost of Mary," Grumpy was scared of ghosts, they thought that would work but grumpy over heard and was not scored mary did not understand how did he know! "Grumpy said how could you, you'll pay for this," he stamped off. What would she do how would she avoid him she knows that she did not have time to tell pa. Pa was in town but she took the chance she got her horse flower. flower was balck with shapes all over that looked like flowers and thay were white and brown mary made it to town safe Grumpy was up in he's room and he naver know she left. Whan she found Pa, Pa came rushing home to wip grumpy grace had been listening for the last couple of days "she asked "Mary if she would forgive her", "Mary said yes". Pa had found Grumpy and Grumpy rushed in and "said he was vary vary sorry and would never ever do tricks again"

that they would have to punish her. She said that Grumpy told a lie, and she showed the books in the dresser. They were not there. She said that she put them there when she came home from school. "I put the books right here!" Then she looked in Grumpy's room, and there they were under Grumpy's bed. Ma and Pa were amazed that Grumpy had done the lie. They were mad, too.

They had to punish him, but how? Mary knew they would act like they never knew! But Grace, she believed Grumpy. How would they convince her? So they had to do something else. But what? In a few days Laura and Carrie, Mary's friends, thought they should play a joke on him. They thought that it was wonderful. But how would they do it? Mary thought they should take his favorite thing, but that was not good enough. So they thought again.

Then they had it. Mary would pretend to be sick, and when Grumpy came in she would jump up right when he was doing the trick, and she would say, "I'm the ghost of Mary." Grumpy was scared of ghosts. They thought that would work. But Grumpy overheard and was not scared. Mary did not understand. How did he know?

Grumpy said, "How could you? You'll pay for this," and stamped off.

What would she do how? Would she avoid him? She knew she did not have time to tell Pa. Pa was in town, but she took the chance. She got her horse, Flower. Flower was black with shapes all over that looked like flowers. They were white and brown. Mary made it to town safe. Grumpy was up in his room, and he never knew she left. When she found Pa, Pa came rushing home to whip Grumpy. Grace had been listening for the last couple of days. She asked Mary if she would forgive her. Mary said yes. Pa had found Grumpy, and Grumpy rushed in and said he was very very sorry and would never ever do tricks again.)

Expository Piece 1

Jupiter, The Great Gas Giant

As you can see I am studying the mechanics of the universe. I had a lot of fun studying about Jupiter. In my report it will tell you about the red spot and moons and rings and interesting facts. I hope you like my report.

By 1951 Jupiter was known to have at least 12 moons. Scientists think Jupiter has 16 or 17 moons, 4 names are Io, Callisto, Ganymede, and Europa. Jupiter's rings are made out of tiny particles.

Jupiters red spot moves up down and sideways. Scientists have studing Jupiter's red spot for more. Than 300 years. the red spot is made out of a red hurricane.

Jupiter years are 12 of our years long. Day 10 hours. Days in a year is 4380. Jupiter is about 500 million miles from the sun. Jupiter is so big that about 1,400 earts could fit inside it. If you put all of the plants together, Jupiter would still be bigger. Did you know it takes less than 10 hours to make one complete turn on its axis. Jupiter is the middle planet. Saturn came withn 25,000 miles of Jupiter. Jupiter is more than 1,400 times bigger than Earth and in another way Jupiter can fit 1,400 Earth inside.

Well I hope you liked my report and you remember it. And don't forget Jupiter is so big it can fit 1,400 Earths inside it. And it is really big.

Expository Piece 2

Rabbits

As you know we have studied living things and I wanted to learn about my rabbit. So here I go.

WHAT IS A RABBIT?

Rabbits are members of the leporid family. All leporids have powerful back feet because when they jump their back feet push and they can jump a long way. And sharp nails to help protect themselves. but the front feet are a little bit different. They are smaller and they are used for a different purpose. They are used to make their houses, called dens. When they make their dends they take their front feet and dig some dirt and push it behind them.

Their teeth on the top have 2 rows. One is for chewing and the other is for grabbing.

If you want a girl, check the rabbit and see if it has nipples. If it does, it might have 8 and it might have 10. It does not matter. (Go to chapter 3 for more information.)

GETTING READY

You will need hay or clay or straw or wood chips or garden dirt. A scraper or a scoop. Food, water, food container, water bottle or bowl. A hutch (go to chapter 4 for more information). In the hutch you well need to have the water bowl or bottle in the cage. And you well need to make sure that the rabbit has water in side or out side.

You need to have your food in the hutch where the rabbit can get it.

Make sure that you have some thing for your rabbit to chew so the rabbit's teeth don't get too long.

You must have enough food for how many rabbits you have. And you have to be old enough to take the responsibility to check the food, play with the rabbit, feed the rabbit and give him water. (Go to chapter 4 for more information.) If you can not be responsible then you should not get one. But if you can get one, don't be disappointed if the rabbit is mean, some are.

CHOOSING YOUR RABBIT

When you see the rabbit you want, point to the rabbit and ask if you can hold the rabbit to see if it is playful. If it is the one you want and it is nice, get it. But if it is not kind then you might think about mating. If you don't want to have babies then get two females because two males will probably fight. If you want two.

If you want to get a baby remember it well grow up and it will be just as adorable. And it is just as easy to fall in love with an adult. When you do pick the one you want ask how big it will get.

If you are going to get it, then ask how you should pick it up. The owner should show you one of these, the football hold or the cradle.

WHAT YOUR RABBIT NEEDS

When you go to feed your rabbit give it hay, something to chew and enough food. You should feed your rabbit at least two times a day. If you have a food container like this one then you only have to worry about if it's full. When you check your rabbit's water make sure it stays at least half full. When you put in something for your rabbit to chew make sure it's not plastic but you can have stuff like an apple tree branch, wooden blocks or hay cubes. If you want to give your rabbit a treat then Cheerios would be good.

THE HUTCH

When you put your rabbit in the place where it will sleep you need to make sure that your rabbit has a comfortable bed and make sure that no animals can get in.

CONCLUSION

Thank you for listening and I hope you learned a lot. It might help you later.

Expository Piece 3

The World of Kenya

You will learn about the geography of Kenya, the animals in Kenya and the people that live in Kenya. So sit back and enjoy the world of Kenya.

The Geography

Kenya is on the east coast of Africa. That is a very long ways away from the U.S. Kenya shares the coast with Tanzania, which is to the south, Uganda which is to the West, Sudan and Ethiopia which are to the North. Kenya is surrounded by all those places, and the ocean.

Kenya is about the size of Texas and slightly bigger than France.

The equator runs though Kenya so it is hot in some places. Northern Kenya is dessert. But still much of Kenya is mountains. The highest mountain in Kenya is 17,058 feet high. That is Mt. Kenya, located east of the highlands.

The second highest mountain is 14,178 feet high Mt. Elgon. Both are higher than Pikes Peak at 14,110 feet. Mt. Elgon is smaller than Longs Peak at 14,255 feet high. Kenya has twin peaks on Mt. Kenya called Batian & Nellon.

Kenya does not have the four seasons that we do. They have two rainy seasons, April - June and October - December. If it does rain, it rains mostly in the morning. In the hot seasons, January - February and then August - September the rivers can dry up, but when it rains they can flood.

The great rift valley is in Kenya also. It starts in the middle east of Kenya and goes 4,000 miles ending at the dead sea.

The Animals

Kenya is famous for their amount of animals. There are 600 species of butterflies and 100 different species of snakes, few are poisonous. The other animals in Kenya are leopards, rhinos, insects, lizards, birds, frogs, alligators, elephants, giraffes, zebras, monkeys and a lot of different kinds of antelope.

The national parks that animals can live in are Aberdare, Amboseli, Lake Nakuru, Masa Mara, Mefu, Mt. Elgon, Narobi, Saiwa Swmp, Sibiloi, Sambury, and Tsauol. They have to police the national parks. The rhino is almost extinct because people kill them for their horns. They also kill crocodiles to make shoes and boots even though it is illegal to kill animals in Kenya!! But they still are alive and there are 40 parks that they can live in. And some animals can survive together and share there eating places.

When some of the people in Kenya go up the cabin on Masi Mara they can see the monkeys eating the junk!!! And the monkeys that eat the junk have a third higher blood pressure then the ones that live on the savanna.

The People

There are 1,000,000 people in Kenya. Most of the 1,000,000 people are Christian and some are Islam. They also believe in spirits and magic. They have religious holidays and special days and things like that too.

Some Kenyans can't understand each other because their languages is different as English is to German. Most of Kenya's people use Kiswahill but some use English and some tribes make there own language.

Most of Kenya's people are farmers. Kenya is made with a hundred different tribes of people. The Bantu tribe is the largest out of the 100 tribes. In the Bantu group the tribes are Luhya, Kambat, Kikuya, Taita, Taweta, Tharaka. The 6 Bantu tribes names are cool. The Kikuya Tribe moved to Mt. Kenya about 400 years ago. Six hundred years ago another tribe moved to Kenya. They are called the Nilotic. They came from Sudan and they are the second biggest group away from the Bantu. Some of the Nilotic Tribe went to lake Victoria to fish and the others became farmers. The tribes in the Nilotic are Ilchamus, Nandi, Poket, Sambarra, Turkana. The Cushitic group is the third largest group and the tribes in that are Boni, & El Molo.

Thanks for listening. I hope you know more than you did before and now you know Kenya is cool.

Expository Piece 4

If I Were President

If I were president, I would be polite, kind, loving and I would help anyone that needs it. If you had a problem I would work it out right away. And if you where sad or mad I would comfort you or help you get over it.

Expository Piece 5

Apollo 13

This is a report on Apollo 13 and you will learn what happened to Apollo 13. Remember that it was launched on April 11, 1970 and the problem started on April 13, 1970.

What are the parts of the space ship? The control module, lunar lander, service module, secondary booster, primary booster.

Two dangers of the space ship are 1, if you had an oxygen tank break you would use up all the oxygen and when you exhaled, the ship would fill up with carbon dioxide and you would die. 2, if a fuel tank leaked and a spark caught it the ship would bow up like the Challenger!

What happened to Apollo 13? Someone had made a mistake when they were making it and it fell apart and an oxygen tank broke and it risked the lives of 3 people. But they did make it back.

How did Apollo 13 get back? There was a man that was going to be the pilot that had to stay on earth because he might get the measles. He heard that they had to make the space ship go farther with hardly any power. So he made it go by shutting down some stuff. They came back and landed in the ocean.

I hope nothing like this happens again.

Curt's five narrative pieces are assessed on the Author's Profile form shown in Figure 5.1; his five expository pieces are assessed on the form in Figure 5.2. For Haley's assessments, see Figures 5.3 and 5.4.

Figure 5.1 Assessment of Curt's Five Narrative Pieces

Author's Profile Rubric

NARRATIVE WRITING
(page 1 of 2)

Author's name: _Curt_

1. Date: _12/94_ Title: _I Went to College_
2. Date: _1/95_ Title: _My Senior Year_
3. Date: _11/95_ Title: _Killer Men_
4. Date: _3/96_ Title: _Christmas_
5. Date: _11/96_ Title: _Mountain Climbing_
6. Date: _____ Title: _____

Storytelling	Nonassessable	Emerging	Developing	Practicing	Proficient	Advanced
Beginning	Piece begins without introduction	Beginning somewhat provides an opening to the story ① ④	Beginning does one of the following: ☐ sets the stage for the story ☐ hooks the reader ☐ moves smoothly into the body of the story	Beginning does two of the following: ☐ sets the stage for the story ☐ hooks the reader ☐ moves smoothly into the body of the story ② ⑤	Beginning does all of the following: ☐ sets the stage for the story ☐ hooks the reader ☐ moves smoothly into the body of the story ③	Beginning does all of the following: ☐ sets the stage for the story ☐ hooks the reader ☐ moves smoothly into the body of the story ☐ is memorable
Character	Characters not used	Words make it somewhat clear about whom the story is written ① ② ③ ④	Main character(s) are clearly: ☐ introduced	Main character(s) are clearly: ☐ introduced ☐ described	Character(s) are revealed (rather than overtly introduced) through action, dialogue, or thought ⑤	Characterization is so strong that the reader comes to know each main character intimately
Setting	Setting not established	Words build some understanding of when and where the story takes place ②	Setting is: ☐ established ① ③	Setting is: ☐ established ☐ clearly described	Setting is: ☐ established ☐ clearly described ☐ believable ④	Setting is so detailed that the reader steps into the world of the story ⑤
Problem	Piece does not build to a problem	A problem is somewhat clear ③	Problem is clearly established ①	Problem is: ☐ well developed through events ②	Problem is: ☐ well developed through events ☐ believable ④ ⑤	Problem is: ☐ well developed through events ☐ believable ☐ complex and memorable
Solution	Problem (if any) is not solved	Words make it somewhat clear how the problem is solved ②	Solution is clearly established ① ③	Solution is: ☐ well developed through events ⑤	Solution is: ☐ well developed through events ☐ believable ④	Solution is: ☐ well developed through events ☐ believable ☐ memorable
Ending	Piece ends without conclusion	Author provides some closure for the piece	Ending: ☐ provides closure ① ② ③ ⑤	Ending: ☐ provides closure ☐ is well developed ④	Ending: ☐ provides closure ☐ is well developed ☐ is believable	Ending: ☐ provides closure ☐ is well developed ☐ is believable ☐ is memorable −3, 4*

* Sometimes one or two of the more advanced indicators are present. They are marked but not circled, showing that the level of development isn't completely attained.

Figure 5.1 (continued)

Author's Profile Rubric

NARRATIVE WRITING
(page 2 of 2)

Language/Style	Nonassessable	Emerging	Developing	Practicing	Proficient	Advanced
Sentence structure	Ideas are decipherable only by the author	Fragments or run-on sentences communicate ideas	In general, sentences: ☐ are correctly structured ①	In general, sentences: ☐ are correctly structured ☐ begin in a variety of ways	In general, sentences: ☐ are correctly structured ☐ begin in a variety of ways ☐ vary in length ② ③ ④ ⑤	In general, sentences: ☐ are correctly structured ☐ begin in a variety of ways ☐ vary in length ☐ include compound and complex forms — 3, 4, 5
Paragraph development	Piece is presented as a set of seemingly disconnected or randomly ordered ideas	Ideas are: ☐ logically ordered ①	Ideas are: ☐ logically ordered ☐ separated into groups ④ ⑤	Paragraphs: ☐ are logically ordered ☐ are indented ☐ begin for each new idea or speaker ② ③	Paragraphs: ☐ are logically ordered ☐ are indented ☐ begin for each new idea or speaker ☐ have topic sentences and supporting details (where appropriate)	Paragraphs: ☐ are logically ordered ☐ are indented ☐ begin for each new idea or speaker ☐ have topic sentences and supporting details (where appropriate) ☐ transition smoothly
Voice	Wording seems to mimic outside sources	Ideas seem to be expressed in the author's own words ①	Language used: ☐ is appropriate for the piece ② ③	Language used: ☐ is appropriate for the piece ☐ is specific and clear	Language used: ☐ is appropriate for the piece ☐ is specific and clear ☐ shows rather than tells ④ ⑤	Language used: ☐ is appropriate for the piece ☐ is specific and clear ☐ shows rather than tells ☐ is distinctly personal

Mechanics	Nonassessable	Emerging	Developing	Practicing	Proficient	Advanced
Punctuation	No punctuation is used	Punctuation is used inconsistently to separate ideas ①	In general, the following punctuation is used correctly: ☐ ending marks ②	In general, the following punctuation is used correctly: ☐ ending marks ☐ apostrophes ☐ commas ③ ④	In general, the following punctuation is used correctly: ☐ ending marks ☐ apostrophes ☐ commas ☐ quotation marks ☐ colons ☐ semicolons ⑤	Punctuation is consistently used to enhance meaning or add effect: ☐ ending marks ☐ apostrophes ☐ commas ☐ quotation marks ☐ colons ☐ semicolons ☐ dashes/hyphens ☐ parentheses ☐ other
Capitalization	All capital, all lowercase, or arbitrarily mixed letters are used	Capital letters are inconsistently used to begin sentences and/or identify proper names ①	In general, the following are capitalized correctly: ☐ sentences ☐ names	In general, the following are capitalized correctly: ☐ sentences ☐ names ☐ titles ② ④	In general, the following are capitalized correctly: ☐ sentences ☐ names ☐ titles ☐ quotations ③ ⑤	In general, the following are capitalized correctly: ☐ sentences ☐ names ☐ titles ☐ quotations ☐ special effects
Spelling	Words are decipherable only by the author	Personal spelling is used with some letter-sound association ①	Enough conventional spelling for easy reading ② ③	Piece is generally spelled conventionally ④ ⑤	Piece is consistently spelled conventionally	Piece is consistently spelled conventionally, even for advanced vocabulary

Figure 5.2 Assessment of Curt's Five Expository Pieces

Author's Profile Rubric

EXPOSITORY WRITING
(page 1 of 2)

Author's name: _Curt_

1. Date: _2/95_ Title: _Jupiter_
2. Date: _9/95_ Title: _Poudre Evergreens_
3. Date: _5/96_ Title: _Battle of Vicksburg_
4. Date: _10/96_ Title: _If I Were President_
5. Date: _3/97_ Title: _Shunda's Newsstand_
6. Date: _____ Title: _____

Structure/ Organization	Nonassessable	Emerging	Developing	Practicing	Proficient	Advanced
Introduction	Piece begins without introduction ②	Author provides hint of an opening ③	Introduction contains the main idea or thesis statement ① ④ ⑤	Introduction contains: ☐ thesis statement ☐ support topics	Introduction contains: ☐ thesis statement ☐ support topics ☐ hook	Introduction contains: ☐ thesis statement ☐ support topics ☐ hook ☐ transition
Body	No support topics are included	Author attempts to develop the thesis or main idea	Body contains at least three support topics ① ② ③ ④ ⑤	Body contains at least three support topics that are: ☐ clearly related to the thesis	Body contains at least three support topics that are: ☐ clearly related to the thesis ☐ in logical order	Body contains at least three support topics that are: ☐ clearly related to the thesis ☐ in logical order ☐ connected with smooth transitions
Conclusion	Piece ends without conclusion ② ④	Author provides some closure	Conclusion contains: ☐ reference to the thesis or main idea ③ ⑤	Conclusion contains: ☐ reference to the thesis or main idea ☐ review of support topics ①	Conclusion contains: ☐ reference to the thesis or main idea ☐ review of support topics ☐ closure techniques	Conclusion contains: ☐ reference to the thesis or main idea ☐ review of support topics ☐ closure techniques ☐ significance of message
Assigned format	No format was given for this assignment ② ③	Piece remotely resembles assigned format	Several elements of assigned format were used	Most elements of assigned format were used	All elements of assigned format were used ① ④ ⑤	Follows assigned format with enhanced presentation

Content	Nonassessable	Emerging	Developing	Practicing	Proficient	Advanced
Thesis statement	Piece is not clearly written about one topic	Main idea may be inferred but is not clearly stated ② ③	Main idea is clearly established in a topic sentence ① ④ ⑤	Thesis statement (or argument) is: ☐ specific ☐ opinion-based	Thesis statement is: ☐ specific ☐ opinion-based ☐ provable	Thesis statement is: ☐ specific ☐ opinion-based ☐ provable ☐ significant
Support topics	No support topics are included	Author attempts to support the thesis or main idea	At least three support topics are included ① ② ③ ④ ⑤	Each support topic: ☐ develops the thesis	Each support topic: ☐ develops the thesis ☐ is believable	Each support topic: ☐ develops the thesis ☐ is believable ☐ creatively examines and connects ideas
Evidence	No evidence is provided to substantiate the support topics	Evidence is occasionally provided to substantiate the support topics	Evidence is provided to substantiate each support topic and is: ☐ relevant ① ② ④ ⑤	Evidence is provided to substantiate each support topic and is: ☐ relevant ☐ documented ③	Evidence is provided to substantiate each support topic and is: ☐ relevant ☐ documented ☐ varied	Evidence is provided to substantiate each support topic and is: ☐ relevant ☐ documented ☐ varied ☐ valid and reliable

Figure 5.2 (continued)

Author's Profile Rubric

EXPOSITORY WRITING
(page 2 of 2)

Language/Style	Nonassessable	Emerging	Developing	Practicing	Proficient	Advanced
Sentence structure	Ideas are decipherable only by the author	Fragments or run-on sentences communicate ideas	In general, sentences: ☐ are correctly structured	In general, sentences: ☐ are correctly structured ☐ begin in a variety of ways ①	In general, sentences: ☐ are correctly structured ☐ begin in a variety of ways ☐ vary in length ② ③ ④ ⑤	In general, sentences: ☐ are correctly structured ☐ begin in a variety of ways ☐ vary in length ☐ include compound and complex forms
Paragraph development	Piece is presented as a set of seemingly disconnected or randomly ordered ideas	Ideas are: ☐ logically ordered ⑤	Ideas are: ☐ logically ordered ☐ separated into groups ①	Paragraphs: ☐ are logically ordered ☐ are indented ☐ begin for each new idea or speaker ② ③ ④	Paragraphs: ☐ are logically ordered ☐ are indented ☐ begin for each new idea or speaker ☐ have topic sentences and supporting details (where appropriate)	Paragraphs: ☐ are logically ordered ☐ are indented ☐ begin for each new idea or speaker ☐ have topic sentences and supporting details (where appropriate) ☐ transition smoothly
Voice	Wording seems to mimic outside sources	Ideas seem to be expressed in the author's own words	Language used: ☐ is appropriate for the piece ① ②	Language used: ☐ is appropriate for the piece ☐ is specific and clear ③ ④ ⑤	Language used: ☐ is appropriate for the piece ☐ is specific and clear ☐ shows rather than tells	Language used: ☐ is appropriate for the piece ☐ is specific and clear ☐ shows rather than tells ☐ is distinctly personal

Mechanics	Nonassessable	Emerging	Developing	Practicing	Proficient	Advanced
Punctuation	No punctuation is used	Punctuation is used inconsistently to separate ideas	In general, the following punctuation is used correctly: ☐ ending marks ① ② ⑤	In general, the following punctuation is used correctly: ☐ ending marks ☐ apostrophes ☐ commas ③ ④	In general, the following punctuation is used correctly: ☐ ending marks ☐ apostrophes ☐ commas ☐ quotation marks ☐ colons ☐ semicolons	Punctuation is consistently used to enhance meaning or add effect: ☐ ending marks ☐ apostrophes ☐ commas ☐ quotation marks ☐ colons ☐ semicolons ☐ dashes/hyphens ☐ parentheses ☐ other
Capitalization	All capital, all lowercase, or arbitrarily mixed letters are used	Capital letters are inconsistently used to begin sentences and/or identify proper names	In general, the following are capitalized correctly: ☐ sentences ☐ names ①	In general, the following are capitalized correctly: ☐ sentences ☐ names ☐ titles ② ③ ④ ⑤	In general, the following are capitalized correctly: ☐ sentences ☐ names ☐ titles ☐ quotations	In general, the following are capitalized correctly: ☐ sentences ☐ names ☐ titles ☐ quotations ☐ special effects
Spelling	Words are decipherable only by the author	Personal spelling is used with some letter-sound association	Enough conventional spelling for easy reading ① ⑤	Piece is generally spelled conventionally ③	Piece is consistently spelled conventionally ②	Piece is consistently spelled conventionally, even for advanced vocabulary ④

Figure 5.3 Assessment of Haley's Five Narrative Pieces

Author's Profile Rubric

NARRATIVE WRITING
(page 1 of 2)

Author's name: _Haley_

1. Date: _1/94_ Title: _Maggie & Haley..._
2. Date: _10/94_ Title: _Haley First Walked_
3. Date: _4/95_ Title: _I Met Breann_
4. Date: _12/95_ Title: _The Houses that Live_
5. Date: _2/96_ Title: _Grumpy Learns His Lesson_
6. Date: _____ Title: _____

Storytelling	Nonassessable	Emerging	Developing	Practicing	Proficient	Advanced
Beginning	Piece begins without introduction ①②	Beginning somewhat provides an opening to the story ③④	Beginning does one of the following: ☐ sets the stage for the story ☐ hooks the reader ☐ moves smoothly into the body of the story ⑤	Beginning does two of the following: ☐ sets the stage for the story ☐ hooks the reader ☐ moves smoothly into the body of the story	Beginning does all of the following: ☐ sets the stage for the story ☐ hooks the reader ☐ moves smoothly into the body of the story	Beginning does all of the following: ☐ sets the stage for the story ☐ hooks the reader ☐ moves smoothly into the body of the story ☐ is memorable
Character	Characters not used	Words make it somewhat clear about whom the story is written ①②④	Main character(s) are clearly: ☐ introduced ③	Main character(s) are clearly: ☐ introduced ☐ described ⑤	Character(s) are revealed (rather than overtly introduced) through action, dialogue, or thought	Characterization is so strong that the reader comes to know each main character intimately
Setting	Setting not established ①②	Words build some understanding of when and where the story takes place ③④⑤	Setting is: ☐ established	Setting is: ☐ established ☐ clearly described	Setting is: ☐ established ☐ clearly described ☐ believable	Setting is so detailed that the reader steps into the world of the story
Problem	Piece does not build to a problem ①②	A problem is somewhat clear ③④	Problem is clearly established	Problem is: ☐ well developed through events ⑤	Problem is: ☐ well developed through events ☐ believable	Problem is: ☐ well developed through events ☐ believable ☐ complex and memorable
Solution	Problem (if any) is not solved ①②	Words make it somewhat clear how the problem is solved ③④	Solution is clearly established ⑤	Solution is: ☐ well developed through events	Solution is: ☐ well developed through events ☐ believable	Solution is: ☐ well developed through events ☐ believable ☐ memorable
Ending	Piece ends without conclusion ①	Author provides some closure for the piece ④	Ending: ☐ provides closure ②③⑤	Ending: ☐ provides closure ☐ is well developed	Ending: ☐ provides closure ☐ is well developed ☐ is believable	Ending: ☐ provides closure ☐ is well developed ☐ is believable ☐ is memorable

Figure 5.3 (continued)

Author's Profile Rubric

NARRATIVE WRITING
(page 2 of 2)

Language/Style	Nonassessable	Emerging	Developing	Practicing	Proficient	Advanced
Sentence structure	Ideas are decipherable only by the author	Fragments or run-on sentences communicate ideas	In general, sentences: ☐ are correctly structured ① ②	In general, sentences: ☐ are correctly structured ☐ begin in a variety of ways ③	In general, sentences: ☐ are correctly structured ☐ begin in a variety of ways ☐ vary in length ④ ⑤	In general, sentences: ☐ are correctly structured ☐ begin in a variety of ways ☐ vary in length ☐ include compound and complex forms
Paragraph development	Piece is presented as a set of seemingly disconnected or randomly ordered ideas ① ②	Ideas are: ☐ logically ordered ③ ④ ⑤	Ideas are: ☐ logically ordered ☐ separated into groups	Paragraphs: ☐ are logically ordered ☐ are indented ☐ begin for each new idea or speaker	Paragraphs: ☐ are logically ordered ☐ are indented ☐ begin for each new idea or speaker ☐ have topic sentences and supporting details (where appropriate)	Paragraphs: ☐ are logically ordered ☐ are indented ☐ begin for each new idea or speaker ☐ have topic sentences and supporting details (where appropriate) ☐ transition smoothly
Voice	Wording seems to mimic outside sources	Ideas seem to be expressed in the author's own words ① ②	Language used: ☐ is appropriate for the piece ③ ④	Language used: ☐ is appropriate for the piece ☐ is specific and clear ⑤	Language used: ☐ is appropriate for the piece ☐ is specific and clear ☐ shows rather than tells	Language used: ☐ is appropriate for the piece ☐ is specific and clear ☐ shows rather than tells ☐ is distinctly personal

Mechanics	Nonassessable	Emerging	Developing	Practicing	Proficient	Advanced
Punctuation	No punctuation is used	Punctuation is used inconsistently to separate ideas ⑤	In general, the following punctuation is used correctly: ☐ ending marks ① ② ③ ④	In general, the following punctuation is used correctly: ☐ ending marks ☐ apostrophes ☐ commas	In general, the following punctuation is used correctly: ☐ ending marks ☐ apostrophes ☐ commas ☐ quotation marks ☐ colons ☐ semicolons	Punctuation is consistently used to enhance meaning or add effect: ☐ ending marks ☐ apostrophes ☐ commas ☐ quotation marks ☐ colons ☐ semicolons ☐ dashes/hyphens ☐ parentheses ☐ other
Capitalization	All capital, all lowercase, or arbitrarily mixed letters are used ① ②	Capital letters are inconsistently used to begin sentences and/or identify proper names ⑤	In general, the following are capitalized correctly: ☐ sentences ☐ names	In general, the following are capitalized correctly: ☐ sentences ☐ names ☐ titles ③ ④	In general, the following are capitalized correctly: ☐ sentences ☐ names ☐ titles ☐ quotations	In general, the following are capitalized correctly: ☐ sentences ☐ names ☐ titles ☐ quotations ☐ special effects
Spelling	Words are decipherable only by the author	Personal spelling is used with some letter-sound association ① ② ③ ④	Enough conventional spelling for easy reading ⑤	Piece is generally spelled conventionally	Piece is consistently spelled conventionally	Piece is consistently spelled conventionally, even for advanced vocabulary

Figure 5.4 Assessment of Haley's Five Expository Pieces

Author's Profile Rubric

EXPOSITORY WRITING
(page 1 of 2)

Author's name: _Haley_

1. Date: _1/95_ Title: _Jupiter: The Great Gas Giant_   4. Date: _9/96_ Title: _If I Were President_
2. Date: _2/96_ Title: _Rabbits_   5. Date: _2/97_ Title: _Apollo 13_
3. Date: _5/96_ Title: _The World of Kenya_   6. Date: _____ Title: _____

Structure/ Organization	Nonassessable	Emerging	Developing	Practicing	Proficient	Advanced
Introduction	Piece begins without introduction	Author provides hint of an opening	Introduction contains the main idea or thesis statement ④ ① ② ③ ⑤	Introduction contains: ☐ thesis statement ☐ support topics	Introduction contains: ☐ thesis statement ☐ support topics ☐ hook	Introduction contains: ☐ thesis statement ☐ support topics ☐ hook ☐ transition
Body	No support topics are included	Author attempts to develop the thesis or main idea ④	Body contains at least three support topics ① ② ③ ⑤	Body contains at least three support topics that are: ☐ clearly related to the thesis	Body contains at least three support topics that are: ☐ clearly related to the thesis ☐ in logical order	Body contains at least three support topics that are: ☐ clearly related to the thesis ☐ in logical order ☐ connected with smooth transitions
Conclusion	Piece ends without conclusion ④	Author provides some closure ① ② ③ ⑤	Conclusion contains: ☐ reference to the thesis or main idea	Conclusion contains: ☐ reference to the thesis or main idea ☐ review of support topics	Conclusion contains: ☐ reference to the thesis or main idea ☐ review of support topics ☐ closure techniques	Conclusion contains: ☐ reference to the thesis or main idea ☐ review of support topics ☐ closure techniques ☐ significance of message
Assigned format	No format was given for this assignment ⑤	Piece remotely resembles assigned format	Several elements of assigned format were used	Most elements of assigned format were used ① ②	All elements of assigned format were used ④	Follows assigned format with enhanced presentation ③

Content	Nonassessable	Emerging	Developing	Practicing	Proficient	Advanced
Thesis statement	Piece is not clearly written about one topic	Main idea may be inferred but is not clearly stated	Main idea is clearly established in a topic sentence ① ② ③ ⑤	Thesis statement (or argument) is: ☐ specific ☐ opinion-based ④	Thesis statement is: ☐ specific ☐ opinion-based ☐ provable	Thesis statement is: ☐ specific ☐ opinion-based ☐ provable ☐ significant
Support topics	No support topics are included	Author attempts to support the thesis or main idea ④	At least three support topics are included ① ② ③ ⑤	Each support topic: ☐ develops the thesis	Each support topic: ☐ develops the thesis ☐ is believable	Each support topic: ☐ develops the thesis ☐ is believable ☐ creatively examines and connects ideas
Evidence	No evidence is provided to substantiate the support topics	Evidence is occasionally provided to substantiate the support topics	Evidence is provided to substantiate each support topic and is: ☐ relevant ① ② ③ ④ ⑤	Evidence is provided to substantiate each support topic and is: ☐ relevant ☐ documented	Evidence is provided to substantiate each support topic and is: ☐ relevant ☐ documented ☐ varied	Evidence is provided to substantiate each support topic and is: ☐ relevant ☐ documented ☐ varied ☐ valid and reliable

Figure 5.4 (continued)

Author's Profile Rubric

EXPOSITORY WRITING
(page 2 of 2)

Language/Style	Nonassessable	Emerging	Developing	Practicing	Proficient	Advanced
Sentence structure	Ideas are decipherable only by the author	Fragments or run-on sentences communicate ideas	In general, sentences: ☐ are correctly structured	In general, sentences: ☐ are correctly structured ☐ begin in a variety of ways	In general, sentences: ☐ are correctly structured ☐ begin in a variety of ways ☐ vary in length ①②③④	In general, sentences: ☐ are correctly structured ☐ begin in a variety of ways ☐ vary in length ☐ include compound and complex forms
Paragraph development	Piece is presented as a set of seemingly disconnected or randomly ordered ideas	Ideas are: ☐ logically ordered ④	Ideas are: ☐ logically ordered ☐ separated into groups ①	Paragraphs: ☐ are logically ordered ☐ are indented ☐ begin for each new idea or speaker	Paragraphs: ☐ are logically ordered ☐ are indented ☐ begin for each new idea or speaker ☐ have topic sentences and supporting details (where ② appropriate) ③	Paragraphs: ☐ are logically ordered ☐ are indented ☐ begin for each new idea or speaker ☐ have topic sentences and supporting details (where appropriate) ☐ transition smoothly
Voice	Wording seems to mimic outside sources	Ideas seem to be expressed in the author's own words	Language used: ☐ is appropriate for the piece	Language used: ☐ is appropriate for the piece ☐ is specific and clear ①②③④	Language used: ☐ is appropriate for the piece ☐ is specific and clear ☐ shows rather than tells	Language used: ☐ is appropriate for the piece ☐ is specific and clear ☐ shows rather than tells ☐ is distinctly personal – 1*

Mechanics	Nonassessable	Emerging	Developing	Practicing	Proficient	Advanced
Punctuation	No punctuation is used	Punctuation is used inconsistently to separate ideas	In general, the following punctuation is used correctly: ☐ ending marks ①② ③④	In general, the following punctuation is used correctly: ☐ ending marks ☐ apostrophes ☐ commas – 1, 2, 3, 4*	In general, the following punctuation is used correctly: ☐ ending marks ☐ apostrophes ☐ commas ☐ quotation marks ☐ colons ☐ semicolons	Punctuation is consistently used to enhance meaning or add effect: ☐ ending marks ☐ apostrophes ☐ commas ☐ quotation marks ☐ colons ☐ semicolons ☐ dashes/hyphens ☐ parentheses ☐ other
Capitalization	All capital, all lowercase, or arbitrarily mixed letters are used	Capital letters are inconsistently used to begin sentences and/or identify proper names	In general, the following are capitalized correctly: ☐ sentences ☐ names ①	In general, the following are capitalized correctly: ☐ sentences ☐ names ☐ titles ②③④	In general, the following are capitalized correctly: ☐ sentences ☐ names ☐ titles ☐ quotations	In general, the following are capitalized correctly: ☐ sentences ☐ names ☐ titles ☐ quotations ☐ special effects
Spelling	Words are decipherable only by the author	Personal spelling is used with some letter-sound association	Enough conventional spelling for easy reading	Piece is generally spelled conventionally ①④	Piece is consistently spelled conventionally ②③	Piece is consistently spelled conventionally, even for advanced vocabulary

* Sometimes one or two of the more advanced indicators are present. They are marked but not circled, showing that the level of development isn't completely attained.

This section contains forms used in the Author's Profile assessment program.

Cover Sheet. The cover sheet may be used when making a formal, one-time assessment on a schoolwide or district-wide basis. It allows teachers to submit a group of writing samples and indicate whatever information the program may request.

The section on special adaptations has a variety of purposes. If students are asked, for example, to produce a writing sample in a certain amount of time with no outside help, not all students will be successful. The district may decide it is better to adapt the process for a given student (allowing a longer time period, special materials, dictation, help with initial ideas, and so forth) than to forego collecting a sample for that student. Such changes in practice may be noted on the sheet.

Other notes that may be written on the cover sheet include notes about whether an assessment should be for only certain tools or skills or if certain ones should not be considered. If requested and approved by the district, ethnic or special needs information may be recorded here as well. This information allows a district to determine if all groups are receiving equal access in writing instruction. If a student, because of sickness or other reasons, is not given the same amount of time to work as others, this should also be noted.

Rubrics for Narrative and Expository Writing. The Author's Profile rubrics for narrative and expository writing are two-sided. The second side (for

Language/Style and Mechanics) is identical for both. A bit of space is allowed at the bottom of each form for any special notes from teacher to student or vice versa.

Some teachers will want to use the form for only one piece. If this is the case, highlighting applicable squares on the rubric will bring more attention to the assessment. If rough draft and final draft are both rated, two different colors are helpful.

Other teachers will use the form for several different pieces to show growth. If this is the case, the titles of the pieces are noted at the top of the rubric and the form is then marked in each category with numbers corresponding to each piece. The numbers may be done in different colors so that the position of each piece may more easily be seen.

Author's Checklists. Three different checklists are included for each type of writing, narrative, or expository. These can be used in several different ways, either by teachers for instructing or assigning specific writing tools, or by students in creating or self-assessing a piece.

Why three different checklists for essentially the same thing? Very young authors may be overwhelmed by a checklist with too much detail; they might benefit most from using Checklist 1. They would then progress to Checklist 2 and then Checklist 3 as more is asked of them. Older authors may begin with Checklist 3, which contains enough detail to provide standards for each line of the rubric. They may move to Checklist 1 as they learn the guidelines in detail and need only a quick reminder of each. All three checklists are appropriate for any piece and may be chosen by teacher or student at any stage of development.

Checklists can also be used by teachers as a guide to instruction. In Checklist 3, for example, each indicator beneath each numbered statement can become a mini-lesson in itself. As writing instruction continues, teachers may choose to rate only writing tools or skills that they have specifically taught. In this case, students may receive with the assignment a sheet on which the items to be assessed are checked. Students are then made aware of what aspect(s) of their writing will receive special attention. Teachers may also use the checklists to informally rate rough drafts. Using the checklists for rough assessments requires less time than using the rubrics, since the decision to be made is simply whether a given skill was used or not, rather than the extent to which it was used.

Authors may also use the checklists to guide their writing. Students may use the checklists in creating a piece, especially if they are readily available or handed out with each assignment. They may use the checklists to self-assess rough drafts and make improvements before handing them in. They may also use the checklists to self-assess their final work, especially if much writing is assigned and a teacher is planning to formally assess only a certain number of pieces.

Cover Letters.   Pages 153 and 154 contain two sample cover letters, one for students and the other for parents. These letters provide more information to students and/or parents about how the Author's Profile is used and what information can be gleaned from it. The letters may be attached to any rated piece of writing sent home.

Cover Sheet for Formal Assessment

Title of piece: _____

Date submitted: _____

Type of piece *(circle one)*:   Narrative   Expository

Author's name: _____

Grade level: _____ Age: _____

Teacher: _____

Advisor *(if different from teacher)*: _____

School: _____

Notes on special adaptations made, if any:

Other notes:

Author's Profile Rubric

NARRATIVE WRITING
(page 1 of 2)

Author's name: _____

1. Date:_____ Title:_____   4. Date:_____ Title:_____
2. Date:_____ Title:_____   5. Date:_____ Title:_____
3. Date:_____ Title:_____   6. Date:_____ Title:_____

Storytelling	Nonassessable	Emerging	Developing	Practicing	Proficient	Advanced
Beginning	Piece begins without introduction	Beginning somewhat provides an opening to the story	Beginning does one of the following: ☐ sets the stage for the story ☐ hooks the reader ☐ moves smoothly into the body of the story	Beginning does two of the following: ☐ sets the stage for the story ☐ hooks the reader ☐ moves smoothly into the body of the story	Beginning does all of the following: ☐ sets the stage for the story ☐ hooks the reader ☐ moves smoothly into the body of the story	Beginning does all of the following: ☐ sets the stage for the story ☐ hooks the reader ☐ moves smoothly into the body of the story ☐ is memorable
Character	Characters not used	Words make it somewhat clear about whom the story is written	Main character(s) are clearly: ☐ introduced	Main character(s) are clearly: ☐ introduced ☐ described	Character(s) are revealed (rather than overtly introduced) through action, dialogue, or thought	Characterization is so strong that the reader comes to know each main character intimately
Setting	Setting not established	Words build some understanding of when and where the story takes place	Setting is: ☐ established	Setting is: ☐ established ☐ clearly described	Setting is: ☐ established ☐ clearly described ☐ believable	Setting is so detailed that the reader steps into the world of the story
Problem	Piece does not build to a problem	A problem is somewhat clear	Problem is clearly established	Problem is: ☐ well developed through events	Problem is: ☐ well developed through events ☐ believable	Problem is: ☐ well developed through events ☐ believable ☐ complex and memorable
Solution	Problem (if any) is not solved	Words make it somewhat clear how the problem is solved	Solution is clearly established	Solution is: ☐ well developed through events	Solution is: ☐ well developed through events ☐ believable	Solution is: ☐ well developed through events ☐ believable ☐ memorable
Ending	Piece ends without conclusion	Author provides some closure for the piece	Ending: ☐ provides closure	Ending: ☐ provides closure ☐ is well developed	Ending: ☐ provides closure ☐ is well developed ☐ is believable	Ending: ☐ provides closure ☐ is well developed ☐ is believable ☐ is memorable

Author's Profile Rubric

NARRATIVE WRITING
(page 2 of 2)

Language/Style	Nonassessable	Emerging	Developing	Practicing	Proficient	Advanced
Sentence structure	Ideas are decipherable only by the author	Fragments or run-on sentences communicate ideas	In general, sentences: ☐ are correctly structured	In general, sentences: ☐ are correctly structured ☐ begin in a variety of ways	In general, sentences: ☐ are correctly structured ☐ begin in a variety of ways ☐ vary in length	In general, sentences: ☐ are correctly structured ☐ begin in a variety of ways ☐ vary in length ☐ include compound and complex forms
Paragraph development	Piece is presented as a set of seemingly disconnected or randomly ordered ideas	Ideas are: ☐ logically ordered	Ideas are: ☐ logically ordered ☐ separated into groups	Paragraphs: ☐ are logically ordered ☐ are indented ☐ begin for each new idea or speaker	Paragraphs: ☐ are logically ordered ☐ are indented ☐ begin for each new idea or speaker ☐ have topic sentences and supporting details (where appropriate)	Paragraphs: ☐ are logically ordered ☐ are indented ☐ begin for each new idea or speaker ☐ have topic sentences and supporting details (where appropriate) ☐ transition smoothly
Voice	Wording seems to mimic outside sources	Ideas seem to be expressed in the author's own words	Language used: ☐ is appropriate for the piece	Language used: ☐ is appropriate for the piece ☐ is specific and clear	Language used: ☐ is appropriate for the piece ☐ is specific and clear ☐ shows rather than tells	Language used: ☐ is appropriate for the piece ☐ is specific and clear ☐ shows rather than tells ☐ is distinctly personal

Mechanics	Nonassessable	Emerging	Developing	Practicing	Proficient	Advanced
Punctuation	No punctuation is used	Punctuation is used inconsistently to separate ideas	In general, the following punctuation is used correctly: ☐ ending marks	In general, the following punctuation is used correctly: ☐ ending marks ☐ apostrophes ☐ commas	In general, the following punctuation is used correctly: ☐ ending marks ☐ apostrophes ☐ commas ☐ quotation marks ☐ colons ☐ semicolons	Punctuation is consistently used to enhance meaning or add effect: ☐ ending marks ☐ apostrophes ☐ commas ☐ quotation marks ☐ colons ☐ semicolons ☐ dashes/hyphens ☐ parentheses ☐ other
Capitalization	All capital, all lowercase, or arbitrarily mixed letters are used	Capital letters are inconsistently used to begin sentences and/or identify proper names	In general, the following are capitalized correctly: ☐ sentences ☐ names	In general, the following are capitalized correctly: ☐ sentences ☐ names ☐ titles	In general, the following are capitalized correctly: ☐ sentences ☐ names ☐ titles ☐ quotations	In general, the following are capitalized correctly: ☐ sentences ☐ names ☐ titles ☐ quotations ☐ special effects
Spelling	Words are decipherable only by the author	Personal spelling is used with some letter-sound association	Enough conventional spelling for easy reading	Piece is generally spelled conventionally	Piece is consistently spelled conventionally	Piece is consistently spelled conventionally, even for advanced vocabulary

Author's Checklist 1

NARRATIVE PIECE

Author's name: _____

Title of piece: _____

Date: _____

Check your story for:

☐ Beginning

☐ Characters

☐ Setting

☐ Problem

☐ Solution

☐ Ending

☐ Your very own words

☐ Order of ideas

☐ Sentences: Check for SPECS…

Subject

Predicate

Ending marks

Capital letters

Spelling

NARRATIVE PIECE

Author's name: _____

Title of piece: _____

Date: _____

Revise and edit your paper for all of the following:

Storytelling

☐ My beginning hooks the reader and sets the stage for the story.

☐ I help my reader get to know my main character(s).

☐ The setting in my story is so detailed and believable that the reader can step into the world of the story.

☐ The problem in my story is well developed, believable, and memorable.

☐ The solution in my story is well developed, believable, and memorable.

☐ My ending provides closure and is believable and memorable.

Language/Style

☐ The sentences in my story are correctly structured, begin in different ways, and are different lengths.

☐ My paragraphs are in order, indented, different for each speaker or idea, and built with main ideas and supporting details.

☐ The language I use is my very own, right for my story and specific and clear. It also shows rather than tells, and sounds especially like me.

Mechanics

☐ In my paper, ending marks, apostrophes, commas, quotation marks, and other types of punctuation are correct.

☐ In my paper, capital letters are used correctly for sentences, names, titles, quotations, and other purposes.

☐ In my paper, all my spelling is correct—even the hard words!

Notes:

NARRATIVE PIECE

Author's name: _____

Title of piece: _____

Date: _____

Storytelling

1. My beginning does all of the following:
   - ☐ sets the stage for the story
   - ☐ hooks the reader
   - ☐ moves smoothly into the story
   - ☐ is memorable
2. My characters are:
   - ☐ revealed through action, dialogue, or thought
   - ☐ easy for my readers to get to know
3. My setting is:
   - ☐ clearly established and described
   - ☐ believable
   - ☐ real enough that the reader steps into the world of the story
4. The problem in my story is:
   - ☐ well developed through events
   - ☐ believable
   - ☐ memorable
5. The solution in my story is:
   - ☐ well developed through events
   - ☐ believable
   - ☐ memorable
6. My ending:
   - ☐ provides closure
   - ☐ is well developed
   - ☐ is believable
   - ☐ is memorable

Notes:

Language/Style

1. My sentences:
   - ☐ are correctly structured
   - ☐ begin in a variety of ways
   - ☐ vary in length
   - ☐ include compound and complex forms
2. My paragraphs:
   - ☐ are logically ordered
   - ☐ are indented
   - ☐ begin for each idea or speaker
   - ☐ have main ideas and supporting details
   - ☐ move smoothly from one to another
3. The language I've used:
   - ☐ is in my own words
   - ☐ is appropriate for my story
   - ☐ is specific and clear
   - ☐ shows rather than tells
   - ☐ sounds like my own way of talking

Mechanics

1. I have used the following punctuation correctly:
   - ☐ ending marks
   - ☐ apostrophes
   - ☐ commas
   - ☐ quotation marks
   - ☐ colons
   - ☐ semicolons
   - ☐ dashes/hyphens
   - ☐ parentheses
   - ☐ other
2. I have used capitalization correctly and effectively for:
   - ☐ sentences
   - ☐ names
   - ☐ titles
   - ☐ quotations
   - ☐ special effects
3. In my paper I have correctly spelled:
   - ☐ all basic words and names
   - ☐ all advanced words

Author's Profile Rubric

EXPOSITORY WRITING
(page 1 of 2)

Author's name: _____

1. Date: _____ Title: _____   4. Date: _____ Title: _____
2. Date: _____ Title: _____   5. Date: _____ Title: _____
3. Date: _____ Title: _____   6. Date: _____ Title: _____

Structure/ Organization	Nonassessable	Emerging	Developing	Practicing	Proficient	Advanced
Introduction	Piece begins without introduction	Author provides hint of an opening	Introduction contains the main idea or thesis statement	Introduction contains: ☐ thesis statement ☐ support topics	Introduction contains: ☐ thesis statement ☐ support topics ☐ hook	Introduction contains: ☐ thesis statement ☐ support topics ☐ hook ☐ transition
Body	No support topics are included	Author attempts to develop the thesis or main idea	Body contains at least three support topics	Body contains at least three support topics that are: ☐ clearly related to the thesis	Body contains at least three support topics that are: ☐ clearly related to the thesis ☐ in logical order	Body contains at least three support topics that are: ☐ clearly related to the thesis ☐ in logical order ☐ connected with smooth transitions
Conclusion	Piece ends without conclusion	Author provides some closure	Conclusion contains: ☐ reference to the thesis or main idea	Conclusion contains: ☐ reference to the thesis or main idea ☐ review of support topics	Conclusion contains: ☐ reference to the thesis or main idea ☐ review of support topics ☐ closure techniques	Conclusion contains: ☐ reference to the thesis or main idea ☐ review of support topics ☐ closure techniques ☐ significance of message
Assigned format	No format was given for this assignment	Piece remotely resembles assigned format	Several elements of assigned format were used	Most elements of assigned format were used	All elements of assigned format were used	Follows assigned format with enhanced presentation

Content	Nonassessable	Emerging	Developing	Practicing	Proficient	Advanced
Thesis statement	Piece is not clearly written about one topic	Main idea may be inferred but is not clearly stated	Main idea is clearly established in a topic sentence	Thesis statement (or argument) is: ☐ specific ☐ opinion-based	Thesis statement is: ☐ specific ☐ opinion-based ☐ provable	Thesis statement is: ☐ specific ☐ opinion-based ☐ provable ☐ significant
Support topics	No support topics are included	Author attempts to support the thesis or main idea	At least three support topics are included	Each support topic: ☐ develops the thesis	Each support topic: ☐ develops the thesis ☐ is believable	Each support topic: ☐ develops the thesis ☐ is believable ☐ creatively examines and connects ideas
Evidence	No evidence is provided to substantiate the support topics	Evidence is occasionally provided to substantiate the support topics	Evidence is provided to substantiate each support topic and is: ☐ relevant	Evidence is provided to substantiate each support topic and is: ☐ relevant ☐ documented	Evidence is provided to substantiate each support topic and is: ☐ relevant ☐ documented ☐ varied	Evidence is provided to substantiate each support topic and is: ☐ relevant ☐ documented ☐ varied ☐ valid and reliable

Author's Profile Rubric

EXPOSITORY WRITING
(page 2 of 2)

Language/Style	Nonassessable	Emerging	Developing	Practicing	Proficient	Advanced
Sentence structure	Ideas are decipherable only by the author	Fragments or run-on sentences communicate ideas	In general, sentences: ☐ are correctly structured	In general, sentences: ☐ are correctly structured ☐ begin in a variety of ways	In general, sentences: ☐ are correctly structured ☐ begin in a variety of ways ☐ vary in length	In general, sentences: ☐ are correctly structured ☐ begin in a variety of ways ☐ vary in length ☐ include compound and complex forms
Paragraph development	Piece is presented as a set of seemingly disconnected or randomly ordered ideas	Ideas are: ☐ logically ordered	Ideas are: ☐ logically ordered ☐ separated into groups	Paragraphs: ☐ are logically ordered ☐ are indented ☐ begin for each new idea or speaker	Paragraphs: ☐ are logically ordered ☐ are indented ☐ begin for each new idea or speaker ☐ have topic sentences and supporting details (where appropriate)	Paragraphs: ☐ are logically ordered ☐ are indented ☐ begin for each new idea or speaker ☐ have topic sentences and supporting details (where appropriate) ☐ transition smoothly
Voice	Wording seems to mimic outside sources	Ideas seem to be expressed in the author's own words	Language used: ☐ is appropriate for the piece	Language used: ☐ is appropriate for the piece ☐ is specific and clear	Language used: ☐ is appropriate for the piece ☐ is specific and clear ☐ shows rather than tells	Language used: ☐ is appropriate for the piece ☐ is specific and clear ☐ shows rather than tells ☐ is distinctly personal

Mechanics	Nonassessable	Emerging	Developing	Practicing	Proficient	Advanced
Punctuation	No punctuation is used	Punctuation is used inconsistently to separate ideas	In general, the following punctuation is used correctly: ☐ ending marks	In general, the following punctuation is used correctly: ☐ ending marks ☐ apostrophes ☐ commas	In general, the following punctuation is used correctly: ☐ ending marks ☐ apostrophes ☐ commas ☐ quotation marks ☐ colons ☐ semicolons	Punctuation is consistently used to enhance meaning or add effect: ☐ ending marks ☐ apostrophes ☐ commas ☐ quotation marks ☐ colons ☐ semicolons ☐ dashes/hyphens ☐ parentheses ☐ other
Capitalization	All capital, all lowercase, or arbitrarily mixed letters are used	Capital letters are inconsistently used to begin sentences and/or identify proper names	In general, the following are capitalized correctly: ☐ sentences ☐ names	In general, the following are capitalized correctly: ☐ sentences ☐ names ☐ titles	In general, the following are capitalized correctly: ☐ sentences ☐ names ☐ titles ☐ quotations	In general, the following are capitalized correctly: ☐ sentences ☐ names ☐ titles ☐ quotations ☐ special effects
Spelling	Words are decipherable only by the author	Personal spelling is used with some letter-sound association	Enough conventional spelling for easy reading	Piece is generally spelled conventionally	Piece is consistently spelled conventionally	Piece is consistently spelled conventionally, even for advanced vocabulary

Author's Checklist 1

EXPOSITORY PIECE

Author's name: _____

Title of piece: _____

Date: _____

Check for:

☐ Introduction

☐ Body

☐ Conclusion

☐ Format

☐ Main idea

☐ Support topics

☐ Evidence

☐ Your very own words

☐ Order of ideas

☐ Sentences: Check for SPECS…

Subject

Predicate

Ending marks

Capital letters

Spelling

EXPOSITORY PIECE

Author's name: _____

Title of piece: _____

Date: _____

Revise and edit your paper for all of the following:

Structure/Organization

☐ My introduction hooks the reader and tells what my paper is about.

☐ The body of my paper has everything my introduction promises in a smooth, understandable order.

☐ My conclusion reviews what my paper was about, provides closure, and tells why my topic is important.

Content

☐ My thesis statement shows what I think about an important topic.

☐ I have at least three support topics that are believable and creative and that help to develop my thesis statement.

☐ From many different, dependable sources, I have provided evidence that substantiates each support topic and is documented in a bibliography.

Language/Style

☐ My sentences are correctly structured, begin in different ways, and are different lengths and types.

☐ My paragraphs are logically ordered, indented, new for each idea, complete with topic sentences and supporting details and connected well.

☐ My language is appropriate for my purpose, is specific and clear, shows rather than tells, and is all my own.

Mechanics

☐ In my paper, ending marks, apostrophes, commas, quotation marks, and other types of punctuation are correct.

☐ In my paper, capital letters are used correctly for sentences, names, titles, quotations, and other purposes.

☐ In my paper, all my spelling is correct.

Notes:

EXPOSITORY PIECE

Author's name: _____

Title of piece: _____

Date: _____

Structure/Organization

1. My introduction contains:
   - ☐ my thesis statement
   - ☐ my support topics
   - ☐ a hook to interest my reader
   - ☐ a smooth transition to the rest of the paper
2. The body of my paper contains at least three support topics that are:
   - ☐ clearly related to my thesis
   - ☐ in logical order
   - ☐ connected with smooth transitions
3. The conclusion of my paper contains:
   - ☐ a reference to my thesis
   - ☐ a review of my support topics
   - ☐ closure technique
   - ☐ the significance of my message
4. My paper:
   - ☐ follows the assigned format
   - ☐ shows that I've enhanced the way it looks

Content

1. My thesis statement is:
   - ☐ specific
   - ☐ opinion-based
   - ☐ provable
   - ☐ significant
2. Each of my support topics:
   - ☐ develops the thesis
   - ☐ is believable
   - ☐ shows creative thinking
3. The evidence I use to substantiate each support topic is:
   - ☐ relevant
   - ☐ documented
   - ☐ varied
   - ☐ valid (factual or proven)
   - ☐ reliable (from appropriate, dependable sources)

Language/Style

1. My sentences:
   - ☐ are correctly structured
   - ☐ begin in a variety of ways
   - ☐ vary in length
   - ☐ include compound and complex forms
2. My paragraphs:
   - ☐ are logically ordered
   - ☐ are indented
   - ☐ begin for each idea or speaker
   - ☐ have main ideas and supporting details
   - ☐ move smoothly from one to another
3. My language:
   - ☐ is my very own
   - ☐ is appropriate for my purpose
   - ☐ is specific and clear
   - ☐ is different and unique

Mechanics

1. In my paper I have used the following punctuation correctly:
   - ☐ ending marks
   - ☐ apostrophes
   - ☐ commas
   - ☐ quotation marks
   - ☐ colons
   - ☐ semicolons
   - ☐ dashes/hyphens
   - ☐ parentheses
   - ☐ other
2. In my paper I have used capitalization correctly for:
   - ☐ sentences
   - ☐ names
   - ☐ titles
   - ☐ quotations
   - ☐ other purposes, such as effect or format
3. In my paper I have correctly spelled:
   - ☐ all basic words and names
   - ☐ all advanced, technical words

Dear Writer,

Attached is your Author's Profile, a formal assessment of your development as a writer. For the assessment, we used a piece you were writing. We assessed the piece at a point after you wrote, edited, and revised, but before you received any specific teacher help (unless noted).

The Author's Profile provides you with levels of development for each writer's skill, for each piece assessed—the form may be used up to six times. You may use it to learn the following about yourself as a writer.

To Learn About...	Look At...
Your current levels of development for each standard	Your highest assessment number (assessments are dated and numbered at the top)
Your growth/progress as a writer (if the table was used to assess more than one piece)	The levels between your earliest and your latest assessment numbers
Your overall level of development in writing	The Author's Profile as a graph—look for general progress toward the right
Your strengths and needs as a writer	The Author's Profile as a graph—those squares marked further to the right are strengths; those marked further to the left are things you may want to work on
Possible goals in writing	Your latest levels of development. Then look to the square immediately to the right of each. This is the step in writing you'll want to strive for next.

Expected levels of development on the Author's Profile vary for different writers, but when reading the assessment, please understand that the Author's Profile was designed to assess *any* author—emerging to professional. Therefore, the highest level (advanced) includes expectations for an adult, accomplished writer, not for a young student writer.

Look at the following table to determine the appropriateness of your levels of development for your level of experience. Keep in mind that this table does not take into account any special needs or circumstances and may need to be adjusted to fit you personally.

Levels of Experience	Primary (5–8 yrs.)	Intermediate (8–11 yrs.)	Middle School (10–14 yrs.)	High School (13–19 yrs.)	College and Beyond (adult)
Expected levels of development	nonassessable emerging developing	nonassessable emerging developing practicing	nonassessable developing practicing proficient	nonassessable practicing proficient advanced	nonassessable proficient advanced

Notice that the "nonassessable" level is included as appropriate in every level of experience. Nonuse of a writing skill may indicate unreadiness, but it may also indicate a choice the author has made about the appropriateness of the skill for this piece. Therefore, if no attempt has been made to use a skill, the piece will simply be labeled nonassessable for that skill. No judgments are made about your level of development for that skill using only evidence from this piece.

Dear Parents,

Attached is your child's Author's Profile, a formal assessment of your child's development as a writer. For the assessment, we used a piece your child was writing. We assessed the piece at a point after he or she wrote, edited, and revised, but before any specific teacher help (unless noted).

The Author's Profile provides levels of development for each writer's skill, for each piece assessed—the form may be used up to six times. You may use it to learn the following about your child as a writer.

To Learn About...	Look At...
Your child's current levels of development for each standard	The location of the highest assessment number (assessments are dated and numbered at the top)
Growth/progress as a writer (if the table was used to assess more than one piece)	The levels between the earliest and latest assessment numbers
Overall level of development in writing	The Author's Profile as a graph—look for general progress toward the right
Strengths and needs as a writer	The Author's Profile as a graph—those squares marked further to the right are strengths; those marked further to the left are things your child may want to work on
Possible goals in writing	Your child's latest levels of development. Then look to the square immediately to the right of each. This is the step in writing your child will want to strive for next.

Expected levels of development on the Author's Profile vary for different writers, but when reading the assessment, please understand that the Author's Profile was designed to assess *any* author—emerging to professional. Therefore, the highest level (advanced) includes expectations for an adult, accomplished writer, not for a young student writer.

Look at the following table to determine the appropriateness of your child's levels of development for his or her level of experience. Keep in mind that this table does not take into account any special needs or circumstances and may need to be adjusted to fit your child personally.

Levels of Experience	Primary (5–8 yrs.)	Intermediate (8–11 yrs.)	Middle School (10–14 yrs.)	High School (13–19 yrs.)	College and Beyond (adult)
Expected levels of development	nonassessable emerging developing	nonassessable emerging developing practicing	nonassessable developing practicing proficient	nonassessable practicing proficient advanced	nonassessable proficient advanced

Notice that the "nonassessable" level is included as appropriate in every level of experience. Nonuse of a writing skill may indicate unreadiness, but it may also indicate a choice the author has made about the appropriateness of the skill for this piece. Therefore, if no attempt has been made to use a skill, the piece will simply be labeled nonassessable for that skill. No judgments are made about your child's level of development for that skill using only evidence from this piece.

Professional Literature

Brooks, J., and M. Brooks. 1993. *The Case for Constructivist Classrooms*. Alexandria, VA: Association for Supervision and Curriculum Development.

Caine, G., and R. Caine. 1991. *Making Connections: Teaching and the Human Brain*. Alexandria, VA: Association for Supervision and Curriculum Development.

Cambourne, Brian. 1988. *The Whole Story: Natural Learning and the Acquisition of Literacy in the Classroom*. Auckland, New Zealand: Ashton Scholastic.

DeFabio, Roseanne Y. 1994 *Outcomes in Process: Setting Standards for Language Use*. Portsmouth, NH: Heinemann.

Fletcher, Ralph. 1993. *What a Writer Needs*. Portsmouth, NH: Heinemann.

Murray, Donald M. 1990. *Write to Learn*. Fort Worth, TX: Holt, Rinehart & Winston.

Routman, Regie. 1994. *Invitations*. Portsmouth, NH: Heinemann.

Taylor, Denny. 1993. *From the Child's Point of View*. Portsmouth, NH: Heinemann.

Turbill, Jan, and Brian Cambourne. 1994. "Assessment in Whole Language Classrooms: Theory into Practice." In *Frameworks: The Theory of Others*. Wollongong, NSW, Australia: Illawarra Technology Corp.

Student Writing

All of the student writing cited in this section was produced at the University of Northern Colorado Laboratory School, Greeley, Colorado.

Alkire, Geoffrey. 1996. "Letter to President Clinton."

Anonymous. 1997. "The Thing."

———. 1996a. "A Map of the Sea."

———. 1996b. "Me and You."

Beaver, Levi. 1995. "Jets."

———. 1996. "The Day Joey and I Went to the Ocean."

———. 1997. "Wolves."

Beaver, Savanna. 1993. "Hickory Dickory Dock."

———. 1996. "Kids Are Crowding Schools."

———. 1997a. "The Apple Revolution."

———. 1997b. "The Little School Bus."

Bedingfield, Beth. 1996. "Louis Pasteur."

Bindel, Luke. 1997. "Voyagers."

Bloskas, Rachel. 1997. "The Poison Dart Frog."

Bunting, Jamie. 1997. "Volleyball."

Collins, Blake. 1997. "Hockey."

Combs, Erin. 1996. "Emily Dickinson: One of the Greatest American Poets of the 19th Century."

———. 1997. "An Account of a Young Child's Life in Germany During World War II."

Combs, Lynn. 1997. "Madonna Amazes Audiences as Evita."

Duran, Rico. 1997 "The Haunted School Bus."

Eberhard, Andy. 1994. "My Dog Dotty."

———. 1995. "Africa."

Femmenino, Eve. 1996. "The Two Dolphins."

Ferguson, Joe. 1997. "Drawing."

Finn, Matt. 1997. "The Lynx Black Cat Irons."

Flanagan, Nicole. 1997a. "Apprentice."

———. 1997b. "Flour Babies."

Flebbe, Ben. 1996a. "My Ride on a Train."

———. 1996b. "Tyrannosaurus Rex."

Forney, Curtis. 1994. "I Went to College."

———. 1995a. "Jupiter."

———. 1995b. "My Senior Year."

———. 1995c. "Poudre Canyon Evergreens."

———. 1996a. "The Battle of Vicksburg."

———. 1996b. "Christmas."

———. 1996c. "If I Were President."

———. 1996d. "Killer Men."

———. 1997a. "Mountain Climbing."

———. 1997b. "Shunda's Newsstand."

———. 1997c. "Wolves."

Gallagher, Emily. 1995. "The Full Moon Fairy."

———. 1997. "Noah's Yacht."

Gietzen, Erica. 1995. "My Sister."

———. 1997. "Andy's Magic Crayons."

Gutierrez, Kathrine. 1996. "Harry the Mountain Goat."

———. 1997. "An Event that Changed My Life."

Huffman, Bryce. 1997. "Wrestling."

Huffman, Clay. 1995. "The Terrible Fishing Trip."

———. 1996. "Boats on the Mississippi."

Jacobs, Jonathan. 1997. "Computers."

Jaramillo, Sadie. 1996. "India's Adventure."

Jimenez, Leo. 1997. "Dancing."

Kalu, Dimma. 1997. "The Adventures of the Crayon Family."

Keil, Melinda. 1997. "The Dolomedes vs. the Argyroneta."

Kershaw, Eli. 1996. "My Dad's First Memory."

Kloberdanz, Anna. 1997. "The Future."

Loew, Erika. 1997. "Poem Analysis: Mother to Son."

Longwell, Kelsey. 1997a. "When I Was Just a Baby."

———. 1997b. "When My Dad Died."

Longwell, Whitney. 1996. "Incas: Children of the Sun."

Martinez, Matt. 1997. "An Event That Changed My Life."

Masterson, Brooks. 1997. "Sears & Roebuck Company: How the Sears Catalogue Linked Rural America."

Morris, Trevor. 1995. "We Went to Sea World."

O'Farrell, Joseph. 1996a. "The Jet."

———. 1996b. "The Sea."

Parra, Kaleb. 1997. "Self Image."

Plasters, Breann. 1995. "The Dolphin Necklace."

———. 1996. "The Story of St. Louis."

Quesenberry, Brendon. 1997. "Honoring African-American Teachers."

Rawlings, Brian. 1996. "The Sea."

Reum, Kalinda. 1997. "Brain Dissection."

Rivera, Adrienne. 1996. "Katie the Bunny."

Rock-Martinez, Jacob. 1996a. "Being a Good Citizen."

———. 1996b. "If I Were President."

Rossman, Haley. 1994. "Maggie and Haley."

———. 1995a. "Haley First Walked."

———. 1995b. "The Houses that Live."

———. 1995c. "Jupiter: The Great Gas Giant."

———. 1995d. "My Trip to the Sand Dunes."

———. 1996a. "Grumpy Learns His Lesson."

———. 1996b. "If I Were President."

———. 1996c. "Rabbits."

———. 1996d. "The World of Kenya."

Sanchez, Bianca. 1996. "The Green Ribbon."

———. 1997. "Snoopy's Adventure."

Sanchez, Marisa. 1997. "The Radio."

Sauer, Brittany. 1996a. "Ducks."

———. 1996b. "Good Leadership."

Sheehan, Connor. 1995a. "Haunted Stadium."

———. 1995b. "Saturn."

———. 1996. "If I Were President."

Shirazi, Matthew. 1995. "Sammy the Squirrel."

Shirazi, Michael. 1996. "The Boat Race."

Shoemaker, Curtis. 1996. "Letter to the President."

Sleight, Ryan. 1997. "The A-10 Thunderbolt."

Solis, Miranda. 1996. "Friends."

———. 1997. "Camping."

Staub, Ben. 1997. "Flour Babies."

Steinway, Jonny. 1996. "Letter to President Clinton."

Stewart, Michelle. 1996. "Letter to the President."

————. 1997. "Brain Dissection."
Stoll, Nikki. 1995. "Super Glen."
Valentine, Mallory. 1995. "The Lost Star."
VanDriel, Mark. 1995. "My First Fall."
Van Wyne, Matt. 1997. "The Television."
Warfield, Liz. 1996. "The Trip Home."
Weber, Andrew. 1996. "Andrew!"
Wendirad, Abebech. 1997. "The Scented Crayons."
Youngren, Kendra. 1997. "Flour Babies."
Zobeck, Katie. 1996a. "Guns are Getting Out of Hand."
————. 1996b. "Nine Stitches."